REALISTIC MODELING FOR TOY TRAINS

— A HI-RAIL GUIDE —

Dennis Brennan

KALMBACH BOOKS

Kalmbach Books
21027 Crossroads Circle
Waukesha, Wisconsin 53186
www.Kalmbach.com/Books

Published in 2009
13 12 11 10 09 1 2 3 4 5

Manufactured in the United States of America

ISBN: 978-0-89024-745-7

Unless noted, photos were taken by the author.

Publisher's Cataloging-In-Publication Data

Brennan, Dennis (Dennis J.)
Realistic modeling for toy trains : a hi-rail guide / Dennis Brennan.

p. : ill. (chiefly col.) ; cm.

ISBN: 978-0-89024-745-7

1. Railroads--Models--Design and construction--Handbooks, manuals, etc.
2. Railroads--Models. 3. Models and modelmaking--Handbooks, manuals, etc. I. Title.

TF197 .B74 2009
625.1/9

CONTENTS

1

What is hi-rail?

This is one of my favorite shots of the Sandy Harbor Terminal Ry., which exemplifies the concept of hi-rail. In this realistic snapshot-like scene, thanks to a well-engineered street underpass, the city bus won't be delayed by the New York Central NW2 switcher on its daily drill to the warehouse district.

I still have the first Lionel Scout set my dad gave me for Christmas so many years ago. His gift was the start of a lifelong hobby that fuels my imagination as much now as it did then. I remember eagerly waiting for the latest Lionel catalog and then getting totally lost in its pages. I could easily see the trains on my 4 x 8 sheet of plywood traveling through that vast artwork-inspired empire.

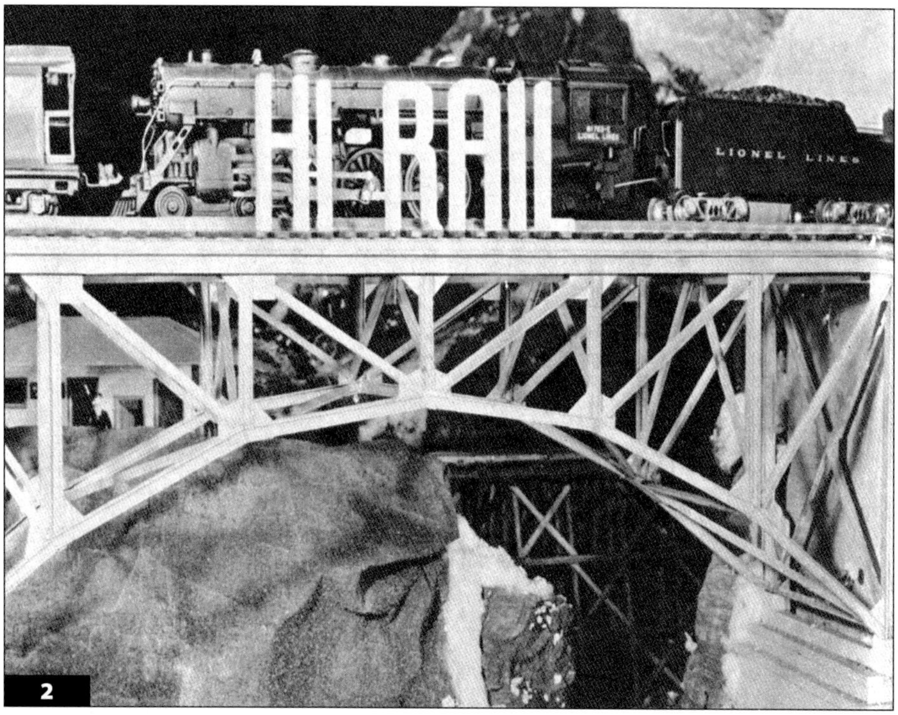

2

The arch bridge came from a kit built by Warren F. Morgan's son. It spans a cutout section of a flattop table. The canyon walls are building paper sprinkled with sawdust. *Photo by Warren F. Morgan*

3

Photos of Lionel's popular postwar layout were regularly featured in advertising, magazines, and books. This was the ultimate three-rail dream layout for many young aspiring model railroaders.

Today, I can give substance to that imagination, bringing those dreams into reality. I classify myself as a hi-railer. Although I use three-rail track, my layout would be considered scale. I don't use any oversized accessories, and I try to make everything look as realistic as possible. While I'm not into timetable operations, my trains usually run with a purpose. I really enjoy setting out and picking up freight cars at various industries. For me, this is what the hobby is all about.

For others, the joy is the toy. I readily admit that a toy train layout has a charm all its own. Reality falls by the wayside with giant gatemen and larger-than-life crossing signals protecting the roadways. Unencumbered by scale fidelity, one is free to play with operating coal loaders, raise a noisy bascule bridge, or place passengers on brightly colored tinplate stations. There is a childlike innocence about such layouts, and therein lies their magic.

There are some hobbyists, however, who are caught between the two ends. They love their toy trains but yearn for something more realistic. Somehow, they just never get there, and their layouts just stagnate. Well, I was one of those people. My first layout never went anywhere because I was too afraid to do anything. When I started on my present layout, I decided to just go for it. I had read all the books and dreamed all the dreams. Over the ensuing years, I've had a lot of fun doing all the things that I'd never done before. In the process, I figured out that it's not all that difficult.

Based on a four-part series published in *Classic Toy Trains* magazine (December 2007 through March 2008), this hi-rail guide is much more than a how-to book on scenery—it's a book on modeling. By using my Sandy Harbor Terminal Ry. as a backdrop, I present a variety of practical tips, tricks, and techniques that can be mastered by anyone. And more importantly, I'll go through my thought processes and show how the various creative elements of a layout fit together. You're welcome to build the hi-rail layout as described, but I encourage you to use it as a springboard for your imagination. So whether you're a toy train novice who doesn't quite know where to begin, a seasoned hi-railer looking for fresh ideas, or someone in between, I think you'll find something of interest.

What is hi-rail?

If you ask 10 people in the hobby what hi-rail is, you'll probably get 10 different answers. One modeler may say, "Any three-rail track layout is hi-rail because the rail is higher than scale rail." Another could define it as the operation of three-rail trains in a realistic setting. And the purist might add, "Except for three-rail track, the layout would be considered scale in terms of scenery, buildings, and equipment."

If you look at the photograph on the opposite page, what makes it seem so realistic? Is it the modeling, the lighting, the composition, the color, or the details? The answer is all of the above. But even more than that—the photo also appears ordinary. It has a snapshot quality, as if taken from a scrapbook of the 1950s, when the photographer just happened to be in the right place at the right time to capture one fleeting moment, **1**.

Trains were only a small part of the realistic tableau presented in Roadside America's display.

Dave Jacobs' O gauge railroad is a fine example of the unlimited variety of settings employed by hi-rail modelers. His stunning Serendip & Western layout recalls a well-worn logging railroad of the old West—and does it all in just 6 x 10 feet.

And that's the beauty of it. The scene that I created and photographed is carefully composed, but it doesn't appear staged. That's because I didn't make a star out of any one element. Initially, your eyes travel from the train down to the bus, then across the tenements to the billboard and back. Only after that initial overview, do you begin to notice the little things. Even then, no single detail holds any more significance than another.

From the luminous, blue sky to the gravel-strewn street, everything looks completely natural. Subtlety is the key. If one particular element calls undue attention to itself, it's overdone. Many modelers mistakenly assume just the opposite. Remember, less is more. The imagination is a powerful tool. Add a few well-placed foreground details, and the mind's eye will fill in the rest. This, to me, is hi-railing at its best and my answer to the question "What is hi-rail?"

A time-honored history

Now, while everyone may not agree on what hi-rail is, most will agree on what hi-rail is not. It's neither the Carpet Central nor the Plywood Pacific. Then, where exactly does the world of toy trains end and the realm of hi-rail begin?

Perhaps the best answer can be found in this excerpt from the article "Converting From Toy to Scale" that first appeared in the 18th annual O-Scale Reference Manual printed in 1951 by Wm. K. Walthers:

When you decide to become a true scale model railroader, you have been convinced that you should discard all of your toy equipment and go whole hog into scale. However, it is not necessary, even at this stage, to abandon your hi-rail track, eliminate the third rail or adopt direct current for propulsion. We have seen many model railroad layouts that will be classed as "scale" yet continue to use the center third rail and alternating current.

Your circular track should be made to a minimum radius of 36 inches. This will permit you to use almost any type of scale freight and passenger cars and many of the scale type locomotives. It is still essential that you standardize on one form of coupler even though you use different types of trucks. In this intermediate stage you are now what is called a hi-railer. You can adopt and use any of the scale type equipment and at the same time continue to use any of your toy accessories. This makes an ideal setup if you are not inclined to go all out for scale.

It's apparent from this passage that the term *hi-rail* was already in common use by 1951. However, the actual origins of *hi-rail* are somewhat obscure, although knowledgeable hobbyists will point to the following passage printed in Warren F. (Frank) Morgan's *The Model Railroad Book*. In this 1954 book, he relates a conversation he had with his sons (referring to himself as Dad) about the layout they were building:

"All right, boys. You win," Dad admitted. We'll go model railroading with 'tinplate' and as much quarter-inch scale equipment as we can adapt to it."

"We ought to have a club," said Jack one night, "with a secret sign, or password, or—or—something." So Dad thought it over—and came up with an idea.

"Well, when I served in World War I they called us 'Rails'—and whenever they saw our shoulder patch, the insignia of the 13th Engineers (Railway), they shouted 'Hi, Rail.' It got to be more or less a common greeting to and between soldier railroaders. What do you say that we use that term, just among us?"

In 1940, Morgan went to Lionel for advice, and the outcome was a two-page story in Lionel's *Model Builder* magazine. When the "Morgan Lines Hi Rail" article appeared in the October 1941 issue, usage of the term *hi-rail* took off, **2**.

Frank Knautz is a traditionalist—no modern-era trains for him. Frank skillfully combines regular Lionel O gauge track, postwar accessories, and first-rate modeling to create a wonderful scene with a 1950s hi-rail sensibility. *Photo by Frank Knautz*

Evolution of hi-rail

In the late 1930s, hobby shops were not much help for the aspiring hi-railer, and many scale modelers felt that they were the only true model railroaders and everyone else was simply playing with toys. But O scale locomotives were not mass produced at that time, so most rolling stock came as craftsman kits. Scratchbuilding was standard. It took a lot of skill to be a scale modeler before World War II, and these hobbyists were justifiably proud of their craftsmanship. Mass-produced, tinplate trains lacking in scale detail and oversize, ready-made accessories just didn't measure up. Adapting scale equipment and models to use with toy trains in a realistic setting was akin to heresy.

The hobby began evolving in the decade before World War II, and eager to tap into the burgeoning O scale market, Lionel changed its image. With the introduction of the 700E scale Hudson in 1937, the company began a welcomed trend towards realism. Lionel's *Model Builder*, also launched in the same year, often featured the work of O scale pioneer Frank Ellison and his famed Delta Lines.

Like Ellison, Frank Morgan wanted to introduce the beginner to the craft side of the hobby, and during the 1940s and '50s, he wrote many articles promoting model railroading with toy train equipment. They appeared in *Model Builder*, *Railroad Model Craftsman*, *Model Railroader*, and *Toy Trains*. Morgan became the reigning authority on the subject, and he was responsible for getting the National Model Railroad Association to officially recognize hi-rail as an accepted form of model railroading.

Lionel's much-publicized postwar New York City showroom layout and the Roadside America tourist attraction in Pennsylvania were both fine examples of early hi-rail layouts, **3** and **4**.

Going forward

Hi-railing is not an exclusive club. Once you decide to add extra ties under your rails, ballast your track, or try your hand at some scenery, you've stepped over the threshold into a new world of modeling. How far you go into it is entirely up to you. As photos **5**, **6**, and **7** show, hi-rail modeling offers a range of approaches. With prophetic words that span more than half a century, Frank Morgan summed it up best in 1954:

It has been many years since the term "hi–rail" was devised and it is still popularly used to identify model railroading with toy train equipment. The problems of the "hi–railer" have become fewer and the opportunities for increased pleasure and achievement have become greater. Anyone who wants to can have a model railroad with a minimum of time, skill, effort, and money. And they can achieve an attractive, realistic appearing, smooth operating railroad in jig–time.

Hopefully, there is something in these chapters for everyone. For those who may be just starting out, I've attempted to demystify the process. If you're an accomplished hi-railer, perhaps you'll discover a new approach. And to the many in between, if this presentation inspires you to expand your horizons, then I will have accomplished my goal. Until next time—all aboard!

On Dick Baker's layout, a Lionel Chesapeake & Ohio streamlined passenger train curls through two reissues of prewar beauties, a Lionel city station and a no. 438 signal tower. The blend of hi-rail and toy-like features borders on perfection.

1-1

Another dimension

A freight train winds around the harbor in this overview of the Sandy Harbor Terminal Ry. You can build this layout or adapt the methods to your own model railroad.

I've had a lot of fun building the Sandy Harbor Terminal Ry., and that's what it's all about. The gritty industrial theme brings back childhood memories of carefree Saturday morning escapades with my best friend, Bobby. Up at the crack of dawn, we would pedal off on a new adventure, and it still amazes me how much fun we could cram in before lunchtime. In today's world of instant gratification, we often get frustrated when it takes more than a few seconds to get to our favorite Internet site. Building a hi-rail layout is a chance to escape the hubbub, get lost in the moment, exercise your creativity, and recall a time when everything was so much simpler.

1-6

On this installed leg pair, notice how the L-girder snugs up against the keeper joist. The cross braces on the legs allow room for the long-way braces below them.

1-7

Braces made out of 1 x 2 lumber and cut at a 45-degree angle help stabilize the benchwork. Gussets made out of ¼" plywood add strength.

1-8

This is the completed L-girder assembly.

Making the framework

Now, you are ready to make the basic framework, **Fig. 3**. First, mark the leg positions on girders A and B as in **Fig. 1**. Leg pair 1 is 30" from the right edge and leg pair 2 is 21" from the left edge. Clamp the two leg pairs to the girders. Adjust the C-clamps so that the top of the girder touches the bottom of each keeper joist. Then drive one screw through the web of the girder into each leg. (When legs and braces are first installed, you need a keeper joist in line with each leg pair. Without it, the framework would collapse. Later, after the table joists are added, these keeper joists can be removed.)

You'll need six 1 x 2 long-way braces between the L-girders and the legs. Make them about 25 percent longer than the legs. I cut mine to 40" with 45-degree angles on the ends. Clamp a brace with attached gusset (an 8" x 8" right triangle cut from ¼" plywood) against the bottom of the leg, **1-7**. The upper end of the brace should rest against the girder web, and the lower end should be about 1" above the bottom of the leg. Drive two screws through the gusset into the leg. If necessary, adjust the leg so it's vertical. Clamp the upper end of the brace and drive a screw into the girder web. Then add screws so there are two at each joint. In the same manner, add a long-way brace to the other leg in the pair.

Following the same procedure, add the second girder (B). This time around, you only need to add a brace to leg pair 1. For added stability, I inserted another L-girder (C) between girders A and B next to leg pair 2. The basic framework for this part of the layout is now complete.

With one section done, the remaining benchwork is easy to do. The big difference is that you add one leg pair to girders D and E and a single support leg to girder D.

Attach leg pair 3, positioning it 30" from the left edge Then attach the other end of girder E to the completed framework section as shown in **Fig. 1**. Simply drive two screws through the web of girder E into the ends of girders A and B.

Next, attach one support leg to girder D. Place the support leg inside the 39¾" mark, so it lines up with the front leg of leg pair 2 from the first lobe. After adding a temporary joist to keep everything aligned, attach 1 x 4 cross braces between the support leg and the front leg of leg pair 2.

Finally, place a 1 x 4 diagonal brace across the bottom of the rear girders to act as a stiffener between the two sections. The basic framework is now finished, **1-8**.

Building the tabletop

The tabletop is built in three sections so that the layout can easily be taken apart without damaging it, **1-9**. Although you could do it with less, I used five sheets of 3⁄16" Luan plywood to cover the tabletop. That way, there's only one seam in each of the two end sections. Figuring out the

Materials and tools

Lumber

Quantity	Item
12	8-foot 1 x 2
20	6-foot 1 x 4
14	8-foot 1 x 4
1	10-foot 1 x 4
4	12-foot 1 x 4
4	8-foot 2 x 4
1	4 x 4 ¼" plywood sheet
5	4 x 8 3⁄16" Luan plywood sheet

Adhesive, foam, and hardware

Quantity	Item
1 gallon	Carpenter's or multipurpose glue
10	4 x 8 sheets of 2" extruded foam insulation
4 pair	2" ball-bearing casters
100	¾" no. 6 coarse thread drywall screw
100	1¼" no. 6 coarse thread drywall screw
24	2½" no. 6 coarse thread drywall screw

Tools

Carpenter's square
C-clamps (6")
Combination square
Countersinking drill bit
Fine-tooth jigsaw blades
Knife-edge jigsaw blades
Phillips-head drill bit
Saber saw or jigsaw
Sanding sponge
Tape measure (15 feet)
Variable-speed cordless drill (9 to 12 volts)

Fig. 2 Leg pair assembly

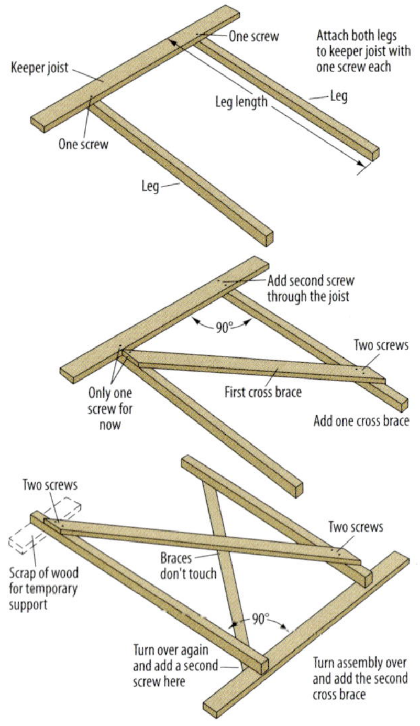

Fig. 3 Framework construction

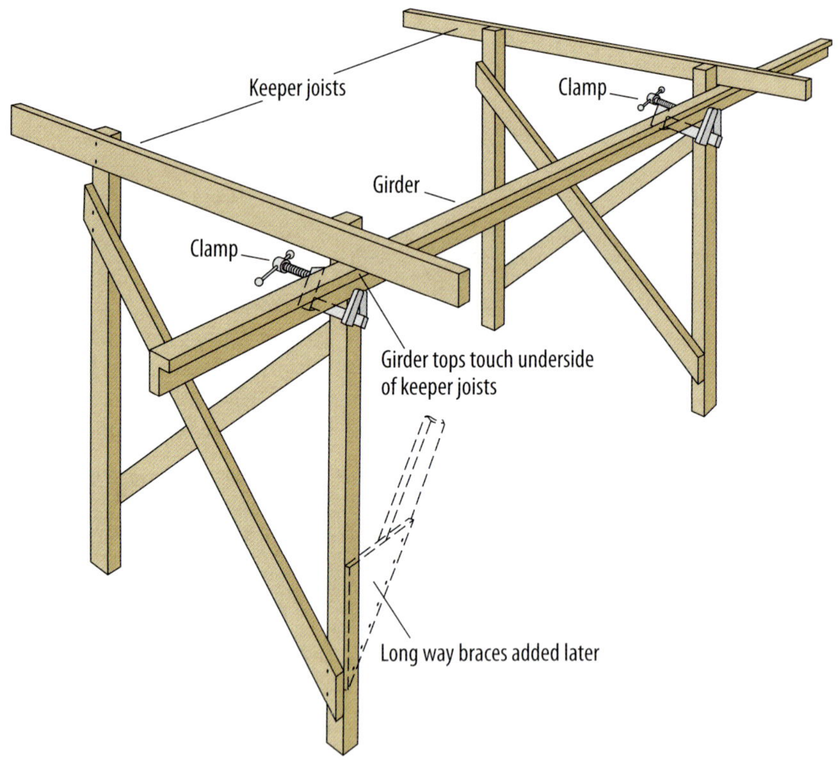

sections was easy—I simply placed a 4 x 8 sheet of plywood lengthwise at each end, squaring it up with the back and the sides of the benchwork. This gave me a 4 x 6-foot middle section.

I placed underlying joists at 24" intervals except in the middle section. Measuring from the outer ends of the girders, working towards the middle, make marks at 2, 4, 6, and 8 feet. Placing two joists back to back at E and J gives you a solid support for each sheet of plywood (**Fig. 4**).

Attach a 1 x 4 x 8 joist flush with, and perpendicular to, the ends of the girders. Then add a 1 x 4 x 8 joist at each of your marks. Use C-clamps to keep everything in alignment, **1-10**. To anchor a joist, simply drive one screw at a slight angle through the girder flange at each end. Once you have the joists positioned, place the 4 x 8 sheets of plywood on top, keeping them in place with a screw in each corner.

To establish the location of the curving edges of the layout, assemble the track on the tabletop and draw the curved outer edges. The dimensions aren't critical but allow as much room as possible for scenery and any structures in front of the track. Also, be sure to give yourself a comfortable aisleway. And if you plan on using under-table switch machines, this is the time to make sure the joists won't interfere with them. It's very easy to reposition a joist at this point, if necessary.

When you're satisfied, remove the track and cut the plywood with a saber saw or jigsaw. Next, put the plywood back on the tabletop, mark the curved edges of the plywood on the joists, and remove the joists for cutting. Normally, once the joists are cut and back in place, you can secure the tabletop, and the benchwork is finished. However, because I wanted to make removable sections, I framed in the joists. I added a 1 x 4 perpendicular to the joists across the back of each section. I also fit 1 x 4 pieces between joists along the abutting seams in the plywood. Finally, I cut and fit pieces along the front.

It was all fairly straightforward. I only had a problem with the angles on one board. My advice is to take your time. Measure carefully and when in doubt—cut it oversize. You can always make it smaller.

Now is also the time to add the remaining support leg under the harbor. I created a pocket for it by sandwiching a 2 x 4 between two 1 x 4s. This arrangement avoids the need for any other bracing. It isn't necessary to add an extra leg to the other side of the layout because it not quite as wide.

Once you're happy with the framework, add the plywood and screw it down on with ¾" screws about 12" apart.

Adding the foam

The last step in completing the tabletop is adding the two layers of 2" foam insulation board. Do one layer at a time and stagger the joints for structural integrity. It's surprising how much the foam increases the rigidity of the tabletop.

First, cut out the front curved sections. Lay a 4 x 8 sheet of foam on top of the plywood and square it up with the side of the tabletop, letting the front hang over the widest part of the layout. Trace the curved outline onto the bottom of the foam and then turn the sheet over to cut it. Make sure the cut line extends beyond the front edge of the layout. Place a wood scrap on top of the foam and temporarily clamp the sheet in position. To make the cut, use a saber saw with a knife blade. It couldn't be simpler.

1-9

The tabletop consists of three sections made from five sheets of plywood. Two 4 x 8 sheets fit lengthwise along the rear of the benchwork. The center sheet is cut to 4 x 6. The other two sheets, extending into the interior, are trimmed and rounded to fit the track.

1-10

C-clamps make it easy to secure a joist while you're attaching it to the L-girder. The vertical C-clamp holds a short piece of 2 x 4 to the L-girder flange. The horizontal C-clamp holds the joist perpendicular.

The knife blade provides a perfectly clean cut without a mess—and no toxic fumes. If you can't find a knife blade, use a fine-tooth metal-cutting blade, which also leaves very little cleanup. And just in case you're considering it, do not use your wife's electric knife. It won't work, and you'll end up buying her a new one. Trust me, I know.

After cutting the front sections, temporarily attach them with a few drywall screws. Then measure and cut the rear strips and the center section. Once the bottom layer of foam is cut, you can glue the middle 4 x 6-foot section and the harbor side to the plywood. Wait to glue foam on the other end of the layout until after cutting out the street underpass (see page 44). In the meantime, you can temporarily secure it with drywall screws.

I used Elmer's carpenter's wood glue, but Elmer's Glue-All works just as well. I do not recommend using the acrylic-based, construction adhesives made for foam application. They are not designed to bond foam to itself, so they are not suitable for our purpose.

The best way to join the foam with the plywood is to trowel the Elmer's over the entire wood surface and then position the foam on top. Use a drywall screw in each corner and a few in the center to keep everything tight. You should also clamp a board along the edges. I also weighted down the sheets with an old set of encyclopedias. Let everything dry overnight and put newspaper on the floor to catch any glue that oozes out from the joint.

The next day you can proceed with the second layer. Remember, you want to overlap the underlying seams within each section. So this time, square up a full sheet with the rear and side of the layout. Again, temporarily use screws to hold the foam in position and butt a second full sheet in front of it. Draw your curved outline along the bottom and then turn it over and cut as before. When you're finished, turn it back over and position it but don't glue it at this point. Again, temporarily use screws to keep it in place.

Assemble the track and use a marker to accurately draw its position on the foam. This is important because the final position of the bascule bridge determines the entrance to the harbor. Everything else flows from that location. Now that we have completed the foundation of the Sandy Harbor, we can move on to trackwork.

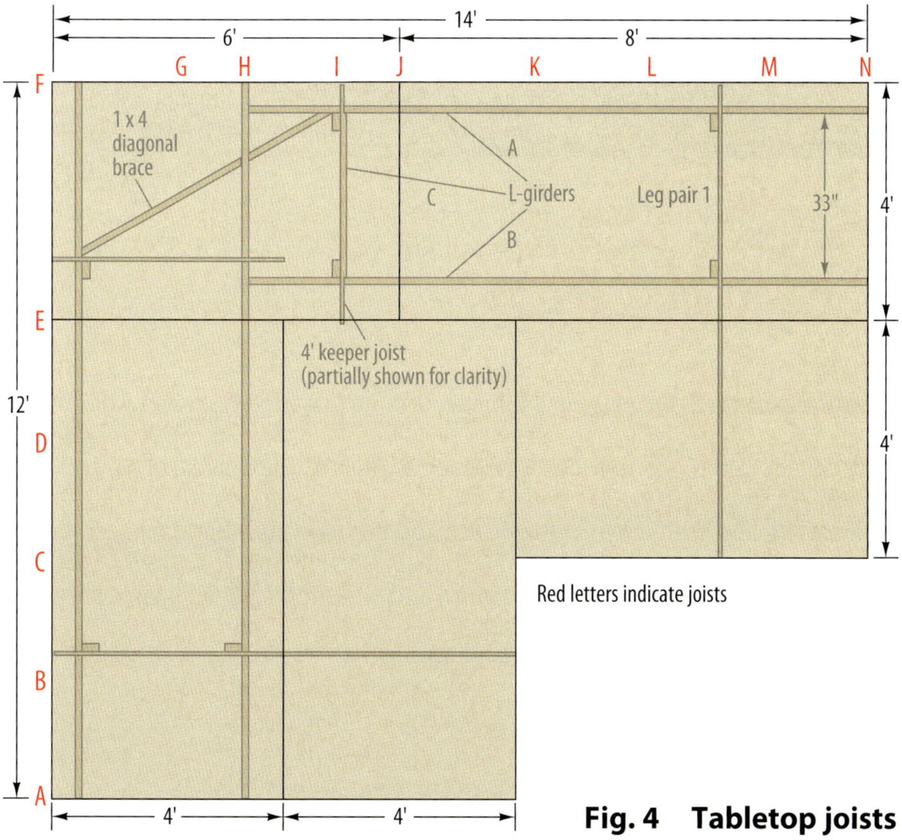

Fig. 4 Tabletop joists

CHAPTER TWO: Laying track

2-1

Making tracks

In this scene, a well-used but serviceable right-of-way deals with a constant shuffling of freight traffic. The day is young as a diminutive NYC docksider sets out for delivery and pickup at the local industries along this realistic-looking stretch of track.

Today, a wide variety of track types is available for running O gauge trains on a hi-rail layout. You are not limited to standard tubular track as Atlas O, GarGraves, MTH, and Ross all make advanced track systems. Whichever track you use, even tubular track, you can make it more realistic through painting, ballasting, and weathering, **2-1**. I'll even show you a way to de-emphasize that ever-present center rail.

2-2 Atlas O track (center) features plastic ties with solid rails. GarGraves (top) track has wood ties with T-shaped tubular rails. MTH Scale Trax has plastic ties with solid rails and a thin black blade for center rail power.

2-4 I prefer to lay my track directly on the foam base. N scale cork keeps the track in place, lowers the ties' profile to scale height, and gives the ballast a natural shoulder. Straight pins secure the cork until the glue dries.

2-3 The Homasote on the left is mated to a ceiling tile on the right. Ordinary masking tape covers the seam. This will all be painted prior to laying the track.

GarGraves flextrack was often the only option for early hi-railers looking for track that was more realistic than tubular track. Introduced in the 1940s, it offered wooden ties and T-shaped rails, and in the '50s, it featured a black "phantom" center rail. Still today, because of its ease of use and reliability, many modelers find GarGraves track with Ross switches an unbeatable combination. This was the choice for serious hi-railers up until the development of track systems by Atlas O and MTH in the 1990s. These systems feature detailed scale ties and solid T rails that are a step above GarGraves' oversized wood ties and tinplate rails, **2-2**. For more on track, see Peter H. Riddle's *Trackwork for Toy Trains* (Kalmbach Books).

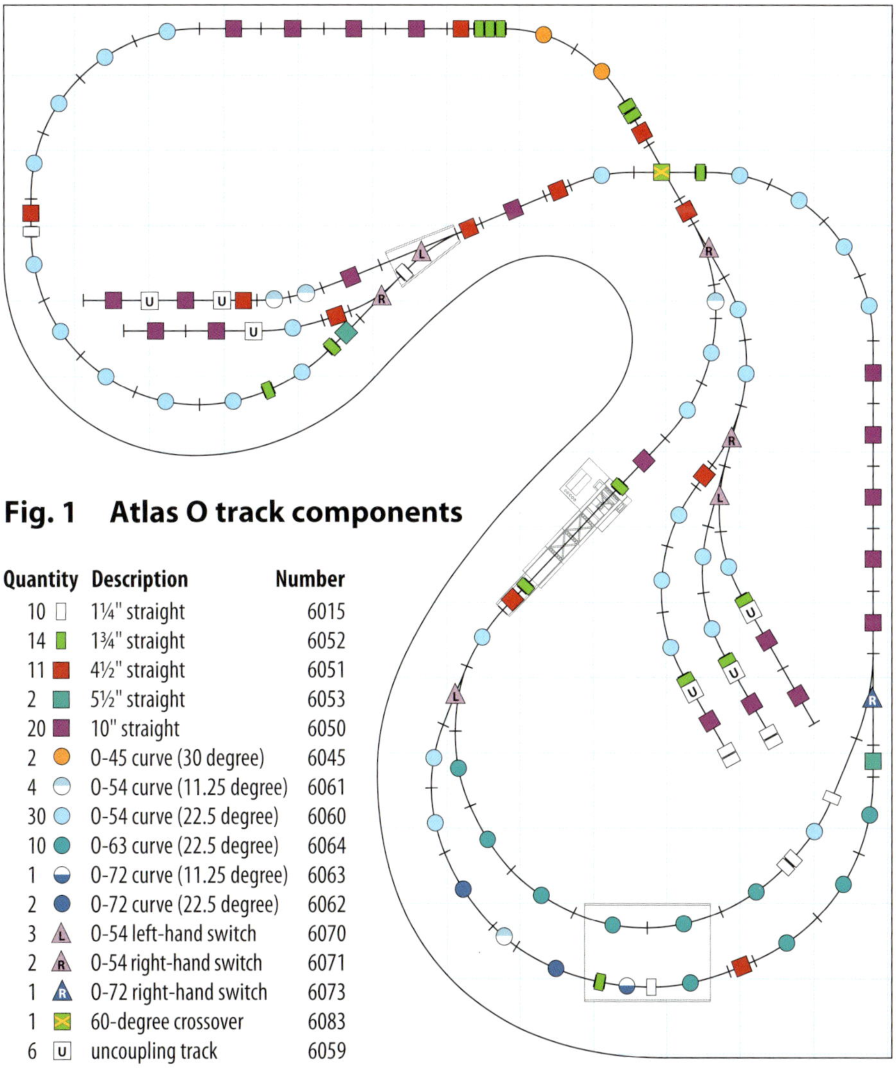

Fig. 1 Atlas O track components

Quantity	Description	Number
10	1¼" straight	6015
14	1¾" straight	6052
11	4½" straight	6051
2	5½" straight	6053
20	10" straight	6050
2	0-45 curve (30 degree)	6045
4	0-54 curve (11.25 degree)	6061
30	0-54 curve (22.5 degree)	6060
10	0-63 curve (22.5 degree)	6064
1	0-72 curve (11.25 degree)	6063
2	0-72 curve (22.5 degree)	6062
3	0-54 left-hand switch	6070
2	0-54 right-hand switch	6071
1	0-72 right-hand switch	6073
1	60-degree crossover	6083
6	uncoupling track	6059

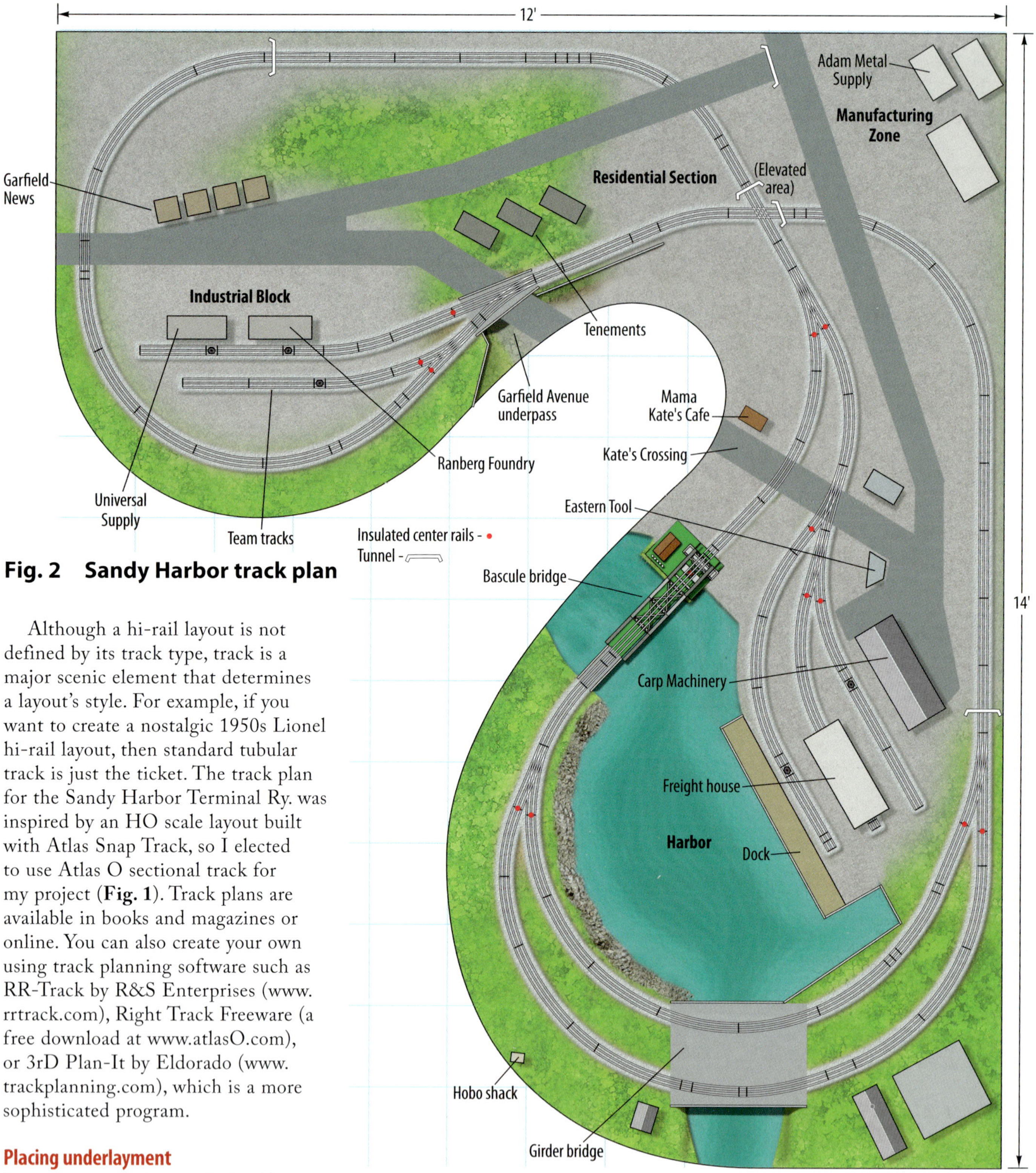

Fig. 2 Sandy Harbor track plan

Although a hi-rail layout is not defined by its track type, track is a major scenic element that determines a layout's style. For example, if you want to create a nostalgic 1950s Lionel hi-rail layout, then standard tubular track is just the ticket. The track plan for the Sandy Harbor Terminal Ry. was inspired by an HO scale layout built with Atlas Snap Track, so I elected to use Atlas O sectional track for my project (**Fig. 1**). Track plans are available in books and magazines or online. You can also create your own using track planning software such as RR-Track by R&S Enterprises (www.rrtrack.com), Right Track Freeware (a free download at www.atlasO.com), or 3rD Plan-It by Eldorado (www.trackplanning.com), which is a more sophisticated program.

Placing underlayment

For quieter operation, track should never be mounted directly to wood. On the Sandy Harbor, I placed two layers of pink construction foam on top of 3⁄16" Luan plywood. This provided great scenic flexibility as well as noise reduction. However, if you're not using foam as a scenery base, I suggest installing Homasote or ceiling tiles between the track and the subroadbed.

Homasote is a dense gray compressed paper material used in building construction for sound or temperature insulation. Since it is no longer in great demand, only major building centers carry it. Because it reduces noise, has a firm surface, and holds screws, model railroaders have been using it for years as a base for scenery and track. Available in 4 x 8-foot sheets, it is usually cut with a wood-cutting blade in a saber saw, which produces an enormous amount of dust. You can eliminate this problem by replacing the wood-cutting blade with a straight knife-edge blade. This blade is also perfect for cutting construction foam and ceiling tile.

Tiles used in suspended ceilings are readily available and cost half as much as Homasote. These panels cut easily with a utility knife, and they can also be carved or sanded. Any style of tile will work, but I prefer using a 2 x 4-foot, plain, flat-surface style such as Armstrong's no. 280. The tile's surface texture isn't critical since I place them face down.

Using Homasote or ceiling tiles under the track is a matter of personal preference. I have used both with equally good results, **2-3**. Homasote may be more durable, but ceiling tiles are more workable. Nevertheless, once the scenery is in place, the difference is negligible. Remember, these materials are not self-supporting and should only be used on top of plywood or other subroadbed material.

After you've glued or screwed the base to your support structure, cover the seams with masking tape. Then seal the surface with a good coat of earth-colored, flat latex wall paint since you'll be using glue and water to bond your ballast and scenery.

Laying track

Once you decide on a track system, follow your track plan (**Fig. 2**) and note any changes you make. As simple as some layout designs, such as the Sandy Harbor, may appear, it can be confusing knowing where each track section belongs if you don't have a plan for reference.

In the process of designing the curving tabletop, the harbor, and the roadway underpass, I joined, separated, and rejoined various sections to form the basic loops. Because of that, it was imperative to use new rail joiners on those pieces during the final assembly, so make sure to have plenty of extra rail joiners (both regular and insulated) on hand. They are inexpensive and make track assembly a smooth process.

The next step may surprise you. After laying the track, I cement N scale cork roadbed along the ties on each side of the track, **2-4**. This little trick serves two purposes. It reduces the profile of the overly tall ties to near-scale height and gives the ballast a natural shoulder. The cork also helps keep the track in place.

Don't worry about screwing your track down, it's not necessary. The glue that secures the ballast also holds the track in place. However, for temporary positioning, I place a drywall screw between two ties, tightening the screw until its head catches the ties.

Make sure you're totally satisfied with your trackwork and its placement before gluing down the cork. When you add scenery, work it up to the edge of the cork roadbed, so the ballast overlaps the scenery for a more natural effect.

Wiring track

Wiring the track is next. Wiring a layout can seem intimidating, but it is often a simple process if you follow a few guidelines. How you control your trains also plays a factor. You can operate them with traditional transformers, Lionel's TrainMaster Command Control, MTH's Digital Command System, or through a combination of methods. If you intend to use MTH's Digital Command System, you may have to wire your layout differently (with star wiring) than when using conventional power or Lionel's TrainMaster Command Control. For a more in-depth look at wiring, see *Wiring Handbook for Toy Trains* and *Command Control for Toy Trains* (Kalmbach Books).

When running trains on an advanced track system, follow these simple measures to ensure a smooth-running layout:

- Use 18 gauge wire for drops and 14 gauge wire for runs
- Run power to tracks on both sides of turnouts and crossings
- Check continuity as you go
- Make a wiring diagram

2-5

The snap lock doesn't provide enough room for the wire attached to the bottom of a terminal joiner. Using a hobby knife, you can notch out the snap-lock to accommodate the wire.

2-6

Power drops come from wires soldered to the bottom of terminal joiners. These are routed through the foam and plywood base using a wire pull made from stiff wire. Drilling the holes isn't hard, but you'll need an extra-long drill bit.

2-7

This is a perfect example of providing track power to both sides of a switch. Notice how the wires are routed off the bridge. The wires on the left skirt a joist. Normally, the wires would drop through holes under the track.

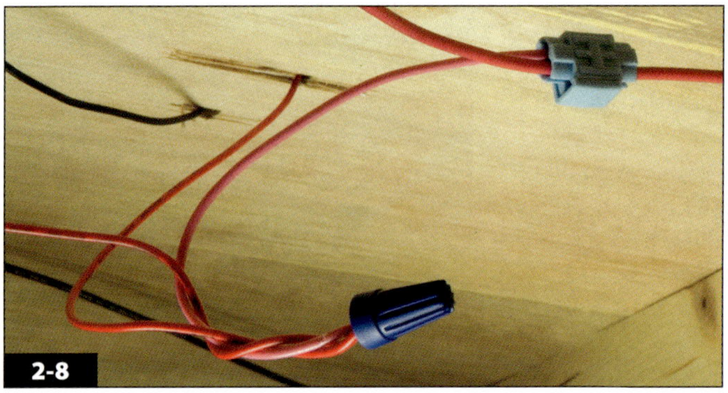

2-8

Press-fit suitcase connectors (light blue) provide a simple way to tap into the 14-gauge feeder line that runs the length of the layout. Wire nuts (dark blue) make it easy to join adjacent power drops.

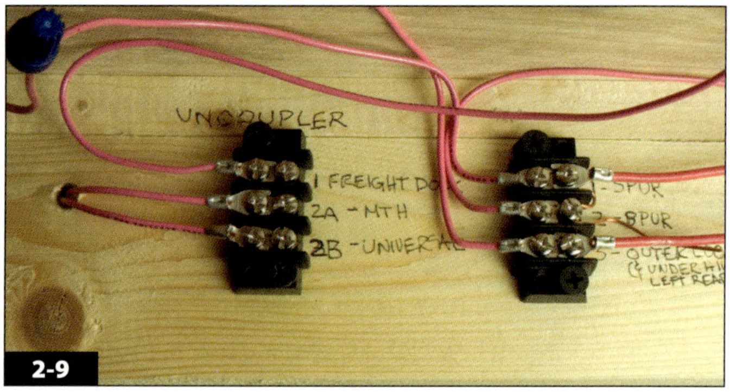

2-9

Terminal strips keep wires organized and offer a convenient place for connections. The right-hand screws on the uncoupler track strip await wires from control panel push buttons.

Power feeds. For power feeds, I rely on easy-to-use Atlas O no. 6090 terminal joiners. These are nothing more than regular metal rail joiners with a short length of electrical wire soldered to the bottom. In a pinch, you can easily make your own. These work well to feed power to the center rail, but when used to connect the outer rails, they can be a bit of a hassle. When using terminal joiners on outer rails, the plastic snap lock interferes with the wire extending below the joiner. The simplest solution is to remove the snap lock using a pair of cutting pliers. The snap locks aren't essential once the track is otherwise secured to the layout. As an alternative, you can cut a notch in each snap lock to accommodate the wire or resolder the wire to the outside of the rail joiner, **2-5**. I also discovered that with certain turnouts, the snap locks wouldn't allow a tight fit. Other than that minor annoyance, the track sections fit together nicely and produce smooth-flowing curves.

Power drops. There are differing opinions and no hard and fast rules regarding where to put power drops and how frequently to space them. Keep in mind that every joint between track pieces is a place for a possible power loss. A good rule of thumb for spacing drops is about every 6 to 8 feet. On a small 4 x 8-foot layout, I would use a minimum of two—one on each end. Naturally, larger layouts should have more. To test, run your most power-hungry train, a lighted passenger set would be ideal, around the layout. Assuming your connections are good, if the train slows down anywhere other than around a curve or going up an incline, then you should add another drop in that area. I don't think you can have too many.

When installing a power drop, I usually drill a hole between the ties adjacent to the terminal joiner. In cases where this might not be practical, such as on a bridge, I'll route the wire off to the side, **2-6**. In either case, the wires will be hidden under the ballast or scenery.

Turnouts and crossings. For those of us who switched to GarGraves track and switches when it was the only alternative to Lionel tubular track, adding power feeds on both sides of a turnout became standard operating procedure, **2-7**. That's because, unlike Lionel switches, center rail power is not continuous through a GarGraves switch. That's still true today and also applies to the regular line of Ross switches. Although Atlas O and MTH Scaletrax do provide electrical continuity through their turnouts, I still recommend adding extra power connections. It can't hurt, and if you're going to have an electrical problem, guess where it's likely to be. Take the extra time now and save yourself the headache of pulling up a switch to fix a broken or loose internal connection sometime in the future.

Connections and continuity. I use press-fit suitcase connectors and wire nuts to attach power drops to the feeder lines that run under the table. A suitcase connector opens up like a suitcase, allowing it to be placed anywhere along an insulated run of wire. It contains a double-slotted metal blade that fits over the main wire (feeder line) and a connecting wire (power drop). If I have several power drops in an area, I'll use a wire nut to tie them together with a single wire that runs to the suitcase connector, **2-8**. This is a quick, simple, and foolproof way to wire your layout. I beg to differ with the assumption that a soldered connection is the only reliable connection. I have been using solderless connectors for more than 20 years and have not yet had a failure. And if wire nuts are good enough for wiring a house, they should be more than adequate for your layout.

Dual-row, screw-type terminals or barrier strips give you a place where you can easily disconnect a turnout or accessory from its control panel switch, **2-9**. By labeling the connections, you'll know where each wire goes. This comes in real handy if you ever have to remove something for servicing.

As you go along, use a multimeter to check electrical connections for continuity. Make sure your trains run well and that your switches work properly. If there are any problems, it is easier to address them now instead of after the track is ballasted.

Insulate any passing sidings, spurs, and individual yard tracks and wire them to on/off toggle switches. Even if you're using command control, you still need tracks that you can power down. You then have places to store conventionally controlled engines, lighted passenger cars, smoking cabooses, and other powered rolling stock.

Wiring diagrams. I can't stress this enough—make a wiring diagram. Even if you know where each wire goes now, in six months, you may not have a clue. Establish a wiring color code and stick with it. I use red for the center rail (hot) and black for the outside rails (common). You can use additional colors for accessories, lights, switch machine power, and other items.

2-10

Before ballasting the track, I use Rust-Oleum Earth Brown Camouflage paint to color the rails. Prior to painting, wipe the rail tops with a paper tower saturated with light oil. Newspaper covers the harbor.

2-11

Without the coating of grease, oil, and engine grime, the rail color is strikingly different on this seldom-used siding. Even so, a dark brown rust color predominates.

Ballasting

At last, you're ready to apply ballast to the track. Ballast is available commercially in a variety of sizes and colors, much of which is too small for O scale. In a quest to find a more reasonable alternative, I discovered a quarried industrial rock made from crushed granite that is accurately scaled and has a prototypical gray color blend. It's called Brennan's Better Ballast, and you can see it on my website: www.brennansmodelrr.com.

With hi-rail track, you can use large quantities of ballast, and over the years, modelers have tried everything from kitty litter to aquarium gravel—all in the quest to save a buck. Unlike your motive power or rolling stock, ballast is a limited expense. The cost to ballast even the largest layout is much less than that of a high-dollar steamer, and you don't have to buy the ballast all at once. As a reference, a 5-pound bag of my ballast will cover 22 feet of GarGraves or Atlas O track. So to ballast 300 feet of track, you would need about 14 bags.

As long as we're on the subject of ballast, here's something else to consider. Some modelers have the mistaken impression that using a rubber-type ballast will help to deaden the sound by absorbing the vibrations. It doesn't. To have that effect, it would have to be applied underneath the track.

Painting the track. To simulate real-looking track, toy train track should be painted. Before ballasting, I spray the track with Rust-Oleum Earth Brown

Loud noises

Back in the 1950s, when I was a boy, part of the fascination with toy trains was their size as well as their sound—and not just the *woo-woo* sound of a whistling tender. I remember being mesmerized by the incessant clickity-clack as my train chased its tail around the 4 x 8-foot layout.

However, in today's high-tech world of command control and engines with sophisticated digital sound systems, it's necessary to minimize mechanical noise. Isolating the track from the tabletop by mounting it on a sound-absorbing material like cork or Homasote is standard operating procedure for many of us. And while that's a good practice, it's only part of the solution.

Since sound is a vibration transmitted through the air as waves, the best way to isolate these waves is through mass. Or more simply, reduce the vibrations to minimize the sound. While this may seem obvious, there are misconceptions on just exactly how to do it.

A friend of mine, who had a large layout, went to great pains to isolate his ballasted Lionel O gauge track from his flat plywood tabletop. He put carpet padding under the track and then fastened the track to the tabletop using screws with rubber grommets under their heads. The grommets were supposed to suppress track vibrations from being transmitted through the screws to the plywood. Yet, when he ran all of his trains, you could hardly hear yourself talk. He then even removed the screws but to no avail.

So what happened? Empty boxcars much like empty barrels amplified the sound, and the expanse of plywood still produced a drum-like resonance. A large, flat plywood tabletop is going to reverberate. You can minimize this by completely covering the table with Homasote or ceiling tiles—not just where the tracks run. You might also consider adding some sound-deadening material underneath the tabletop. Using open grid or L-girder benchwork to support your track on individual risers also reduces vibration.

The acoustics of your train room is also a factor. If there is no carpet, drapes, or furniture, much of the sound will bounce off the walls, floor, and ceiling and create an echo effect. While you may not be able to put padding on your walls, hanging layout skirting and laying carpeting will help tone down the sound.

2-12

For applying liquids, an applicator bottle is much easier to use and far more precise than either a spray bottle or turkey baster. After soaking the ballast with wet water, the bonding solution flows easily between the ties.

2-13

Well-used tracks in Kansas City's West Bottoms warehouse district show a siding on the left and a main line on the right. Note the discoloration of the ballast due to grime and weathering.

2-14

Here's an example of mainline tracks on the outskirts of Kansas City. The ties appear to be in slightly better condition then those in the West Bottoms.

Camouflage spray paint (no. 1918830), **2-10**. As they are exposed to the elements, rails eventually rust to a mostly dark-brown color. The rails are also colored by grease and grime from the engines and railcars that travel upon them, **2-11**. Mainline rails, such as the track on the Sandy Harbor, tend to be dull brown while seldom used sidings are a bit brighter.

Prior to painting, wipe the rail tops with a paper tower saturated with a lubricant or light oil. I used silicone clipper lube because that's what I had, but any silicone spray lube should work. The paint won't adhere to the coated surface, so removing excess paint is as simple as wiping it off. Spray about six feet of track at a time and then wipe off the rails. Remember, the foam must be sealed with latex paint before spraying. Otherwise, the solvent in the spray paint will eat the foam.

Spraying the track covers all three rails and gets rid of the plastic sheen on the ties. And contrary to popular belief, a black center rail doesn't make it less noticeable—quite the opposite. The center rail on Atlas track has tie plates and is identical to the outside rails. Leaving it black will only make it stand out.

If your track is already ballasted, you can brush on some decanted spray paint. The paint dries fast, so only decant enough into a small glass bowl to work on one section at a time. Then drag a loaded no. 4 artist brush along the side of the rail. Have a jar of paint thinner handy to keep your brush from getting stiff. The painting goes fast since you only need to paint the sides of the rails that are visible. Also, don't worry if you get some paint on the ties. It only adds to the weathering effect.

Adding the ballast. Applying the ballast is a time-consuming process, so it is better to work on a 3-foot section at a time. Distribute the ballast between the rails with a paper cup and then spread it out with a ¾"-wide, stiff-bristle brush. Work the ballast down between the ties, making it level with the tie tops. Now, gently tap a wood block along the top of the rails. This action will impart a natural crown to the ballast. Don't leave any granules on the ties.

Next, spread ballast on the outside of the rails, closely following the contour of the cork. For a natural look, vary the depth of the ballast around the ends of a few ties. When you're satisfied, use an applicator bottle to soak the ballast with "wet water" (water with a few drops of dish detergent added). This soaking agent reduces the surface tension of water and allows the glue to be easily absorbed and evenly distributed throughout the ballast. If you don't use detergent or another soaking agent, the bonding solution will just ball up on top of the ballast.

For a bonding solution, I mix one part white glue, one part earth-colored latex paint, and one part water in an applicator bottle. The paint in the solution kills any sheen on the ballast, which eliminates that freshly ballasted look. Completely soak the ballast with the bonding solution to the saturation point, **2-12**. Don't worry if some of the mixture gets on a tie here and there. Again, it only adds to the weathering. I keep a paper towel handy to blot up excessive amounts. Be careful around any turnouts because glue and ballast can interfere with their proper operation.

Finally, without disturbing the ballast, carefully wipe the top of the rails with a damp cloth to pick up any stray glue. Let the glue dry overnight and then vacuum the track thoroughly to remove any loose ballast. Crushed rock or soil may contain magnetic particles that could be attracted to locomotive wheels, gears, and motors and damage these parts.

Weathering

Track and ballast are subject to the same effects of water, dirt, grime, and rust as is everything else on your layout, **2-13**. Here are some general thoughts to keep in mind when weathering track. A heavily used mainline track will exhibit more grime between the rails than a lightly used siding or spur, **2-14**. The colors of the ballast and the dirt tend to blend into one another. Also, a spur may have little or no ballast and can be almost buried in the dirt. The secret for creating a natural look is to avoid uniformity. To really see what I'm talking about, take some pictures of local tracks. I'm often amazed at the some of the details I discover when I go out with camera in hand.

Now that we've gone over some weathering principles, let's get to the actual weathering. After the ballast dries, it still might look too clean, so let's dirty it up with a basic earth wash. Mix two parts water with one part earth-colored latex paint and then flow this mixture over the ballast using an applicator bottle. Don't be afraid to let some of this color creep into the dirt or weeds along the ballast shoulder. This is where blending comes in. Vary the amount of the ballast—heavier in some spots and lighter in others. Let the ballast dry before evaluating the results. Remember, you can always add more.

Next, add some grime. Mix ¾ teaspoon India ink with 8 ounces of the earth wash described above. This produces a great grungy brown color. Drizzle it between the ties, both inside and outside the rails. The heaviest concentration should be inside the track. Dampen the ballast shoulders and adjacent ground with wet water. Randomly dribble the grungy wash on the ballast shoulders, letting it mix and blend with the surrounding terrain in various places. If you overdo an area, just add some more wet water.

Finishing the track

To finish weathering your track, a little chalk work is in order. I only finish areas that are easily viewed, such as ties and rail sides, and it's not as tedious a process as you might think. This final touch results in a subtle, realistic weathered appearance, **2-15**.

For finishing ties, I found that a mix of basic colors produces the best results. I like to use light brown, dark brown, light gray, and dark gray. You can experiment on a spare piece of track to find the colors you prefer. Select one color, lightly rub the chalk stick on random ties, and spread it out with your finger. Then add your remaining colors to other ties but, for variety, leave some unfinished. Once the ties have one coat of chalk, go back and blend in additional colors in varying patterns, **2-16**.

Next, randomly streak the rail sides with light yellow chalk to duplicate the rust patterns seen in photo **2-11**. To do this, I rub a cosmetic applicator (similar to a cotton swab) on the chalk stick and apply vertical streaks on the rails, **2-17**. Then add just a bit of brown in places and feather the chalk marks out with a regular paintbrush.

After completing these final touches, we can look at creating the harbor scene, the focal point of the layout, in chapter 3.

2-15

What a difference! The black center rail and plastic ties clearly stand out when they're not painted (left). The weathered rails look much more realistic (right).

2-16

Can you believe these ties are plastic? This passing siding on the Sandy Harbor shows how painting the track and then selectively coloring the ties with chalk adds a subtle, realistic variation.

2-17

Weathering the rails is as easy as applying streaks of light yellow chalk and brushing it out.

3-1

Water, water, everywhere

With a bascule bridge, spur track, and gantry crane, Sandy Harbor's harbor provides many operational activities.

Nothing conjures up images of big-time railroading better than a bustling harbor scene. In this chapter, I'll describe how I created the waterfront on the Sandy Harbor Terminal Ry. Crafting a scene like this is not that difficult, and it provides plenty of operational possibilities, **3-1**. The biggest feature is the water, and it couldn't be simpler to create. But I'm getting ahead of myself. Before adding the water, you have to set up the harbor.

Laying out the harbor scene

The Lionel bascule bridge identifies the entrance to the harbor, and the pier's railroad spur defines the dock area. When planning the harbor, I allowed 6" from the center rail of the dock spur to the front of the 30"-long dock that lines up with the end of the track. The 6" measurement is determined by the reach of the Lionel gantry crane. The little slip beyond the dock is 7" wide.

Before marking the top layer of extruded foam, temporarily outline the entire harbor area with masking tape. The tape is easy to reposition as you figure things out. On the right side of the harbor, I roughed in the rocky shoreline across from the dock.

Once you are satisfied with the arrangement, outline the harbor with a marker, using the tape as a guide. If in doubt, leave in extra foam—just as I did with the shoreline. It is simple enough to later cut away excess foam. On the other hand, it is just as easy to put some foam back. So don't worry too much about it. That's the beauty of working with foam.

Next, remove the track and cut out the harbor from the top layer of foam, **3-2**. I used a saber saw with a knife-edge blade, and since this upper layer was still loose, I did the cutting away from the tabletop. I then sealed the base of the harbor (the bottom foam layer) with my standard earth-colored latex paint, but you can use any latex or water-based paint to seal the harbor basin. (I use Glidden no. 90YR 15/193 as a base coat under all my scenery.) After letting the base coat dry thoroughly, I sprayed the harbor basin with Rust-Oleum Deep Forest Green Camouflage paint (no. 1919). The latex paint forms a barrier that keeps the spray paint from attacking the foam. Once that had dried, I replaced the surrounding foam landforms and reassembled the sections of track. Now the layout was ready for the water.

The harbor has been cut out of the top layer of foam. The foam will be cut back and rocks added. Temporary foam bridges support the tracks in the foreground.

There is a clear difference between the painted glass (top) and unpainted glass. Painting the back of the glass causes the glass to act like a mirror.

Creating the water

There are many ways to create water: two-part epoxy coatings, polyester casting resins, high gloss varnish, acrylic gloss medium, Plexiglas, and glass. Woodland Scenics also offers several pourable water-modeling products. But many of these techniques are better suited for smaller applications. Because the harbor takes up a relatively large amount of space (approximately 3 x 8 feet), I decided to use a patterned piece of glass for the water. I chose a brand called Aquatex that is mainly used for shower doors and patio tables and is available from large retail glass suppliers.

To create the water, I simply spray-painted the bottom side of the glass and then set it in place. It is truly that simple,

The color of water and concrete

A shallow stream like Rock Creek is more transparent than reflective. The tiny hint of blue in the background comes from the sky.

The Little Blue River should be called the Muddy Brown River. The deep, murky water is clearly defined by its reflections.

The rough concrete texture results more from a mottled appearance than an actual bumpy surface.

The varied colors of the old concrete bridge differ from the newer light gray pavement (right). The asphalt shows two different shades of gray, demonstrating that streets are not often black.

Should modeled water be clear? That depends on what you're trying to depict. A shallow, boulder-strewn stream does not look realistic rendered as bright blue, **1**. It's probably best left clear. For the harbor, I settled on a nondescript green base color that perfectly depicts the grungy atmosphere of a busy manufacturing area. Its color comes from the reflections and the sky (a white backdrop with blue light focused on it).

Much has been written over the years about the proper color for modeled water. Here's my take on the subject. Water itself is colorless. The color you see on its surface is the color of the surroundings. Deep water found in an industrial harbor appears murky when you peer into it. If you look across its surface, you'll see a larger area of sky and more of its environs reflected. Water color changes with the sky color, with its surroundings, and with your particular vantage point.

I know this may fly in the face of the widely held tenets about modeling water, but as the water on my Sandy River layout shows, the realistic depiction of a large body of water is all about undulating reflections, **2**. It has nothing to do with transparency, the color blue, or even the idea that it should be darker at its center.

Concrete is also a challenge. First, don't be concerned about duplicating texture, **3**. I have used nothing more than foam core painted with regular (not textured) spray paint. And second, there is no single absolute color for it. Colors can vary from a light gray (new concrete) through a dark cardboard tan (old concrete). And even then, the surface colors will vary due to stains and weathering. So the color of concrete depends on what you are modeling, **4**. My suggestion is to go out and take photos of concrete sidewalks, foundations, retaining walls, and bridges. You'll be surprised at how many color variances you will find.

For a basic aged-concrete color I use two different methods. One uses acrylic tube paint with this formula: two parts Medium Gray mixed with one part Raw Sienna.

The other is my own discovery: Uline's tan Maskout spray paint (S-249) that is used for covering the markings on cardboard boxes. For a different look, I'll build up the color by lightly misting the surface first with flat white, gray primer, and the tan Maskout paint, letting the previous applications show through. The idea is to create a mottled appearance by varying the colors and their density across the surface. Maskout paint is available on Uline's Web site, www.uline.com.

and the final result speaks for itself. As a bonus, the glass is easy to clean, and you don't have to worry about scratching or dulling the surface.

This patterned glass has two different surfaces, with the ripples being more distinct on one side. I know it seems counterintuitive, but I used the more heavily rippled side as the bottom. The smoother top surface looks more natural.

One of my main concerns about using a solid rippled surface was that the pilings, boats, retaining walls, and rocks would appear to be sitting on top of the water rather than in it. However, the ripples in the glass are so shallow that there were no obvious gaps, and the reflections pull everything down into the water, so transparency is not an issue.

To size the glass, I made a template of the harbor area using a roll of white banner paper. It wasn't wide enough, so I taped three pieces together and placed them in the basin. After sliding the paper under the foam, I traced the outline of the harbor with a marker. Then I removed the paper, cut along the lines, and took the template to the glass company, so they could cut the glass. I made sure the glasscutter knew the smoother surface would face up.

Although the template follows the shape of the harbor, I had the glass cut straight to the largest dimensions to minimize weak areas at the corners. The 3⁄16"-thick glass came in a 60" x 84" sheet. Since the harbor is about 96" long, I had to have the glass cut into two pieces, so it would fit lengthwise. Fortunately, I could hide the seam under the girder bridge that spans the outlet. To make the glass safer, I had the edges beveled except along the seam. However, it wasn't necessary to have the glass tempered since it would be lying flat and supported by 2" of foam.

I spray-painted the bottom side of the glass with Rust-Oleum Deep Forest Green Camouflage, **3-3**. I sprayed on several light coats for a smooth, even look. If you place white paper under the glass, you can check the finish. Painting is a critical step, and you can't rush the process. I suggest painting the foam underneath the glass the same color because the paint can easily be scraped off when handling the glass.

After letting the paint cure for several days, I had a friend help me install the pieces of glass. Before placing the glass, I thoroughly vacuumed the harbor bed. We then set the pieces down as close as possible to their final position, carefully jockeying them into place to avoid scraping off any paint.

3-4

The square pieces of plywood serve as screw anchors. Similar pieces on the upper layer of foam provide a simple way to secure it. This makes it easy to remove if necessary. The upper layer of foam will sit on top of the glass, not beside it.

To lock the glass in position, I used some 3⁄16"-thick pieces of foam core as spacers and pieces of plywood for screw anchor points, **3-4**. I secured the foam core and wood to the foam with white glue.

The dock module

Because of its location, I decided to build the dock area as a separate module, **3-5**. This was the only space that would be impractical to finish in place on the layout. I made sure I had accurately placed and outlined the sections of track before removing the foam. I completed all of the wiring and most of the scenery, including the ballast, at my work table. Since I could reach the back of the module from the rear of the layout, I left that part for later.

The wiring included power and common leads to each of the three insulated sidings and power leads to the uncoupling magnets. Also, as standard operating procedure, I ran power leads to the approach and both branches of each turnout. I can't stress enough how important this is. You should never rely on a turnout to pass power down the line. (See pages 17-18 for more on wiring.)

I resisted the urge to use a single material to surround the harbor, so there are wooden pilings and a metal seawall to the left of the dock. Using wood, stone, metal, and concrete to meet the water's edge adds more visual interest and greatly expands the scene.

The dock and sea walls are made from easily obtainable materials. In addition to my local hobby shop, I frequent places like Hobby Lobby and Jo-Ann Fabric. Both have extensive crafting and scrapbooking departments. And if you haven't yet checked out scrapbooking supplies, I suggest you run to your nearest store. There is a treasure trove of interesting materials for your modeling pleasure—paper sheets with printed designs suitable for wallpaper, packages of fluted cardboard to make corrugated metal siding, 3-D letters for signs, and a host of odd doodads whose use is only limited by your imagination.

Making the dock

The dock represents a concrete structure faced with horizontal boards attached to pilings along the apron, **3-6**. Although its construction was a little more involved than the simple wood-piling wall I used elsewhere, it features a distinctive look. I started construction by covering the foam insulation with foam core. I then added a second layer of foam core, securing it with white glue, to make it level with the rails. Next, I embossed expansion joints

3-5

The turnout and the three sidings make up the dock module. The brown-painted area delineates its shape. Here, I've temporarily set it back in place to check the track alignment before finishing the scenery at my workbench. Note the four screw anchors.

3-6

I based the wooden dock design on those I found in the two volumes of *New York Harbor Railroads In Color*.

into the deck with a dull pencil, being careful not to push through the surface into the foam.

I sprayed the concrete areas first with gray primer and then with Uline tan Maskout paint (no. S-249). I then lightly sanded the deck with a fine-grade sanding sponge, stopping when just a hint of the underlying gray started to show through. Wooden ties placed alongside the rails made the surface level with the concrete on both sides of the track. I added a strip of pink foam covered with foam core to expand the dock apron.

The preliminary work of cutting and staining took much longer than the actual assembly. For the wooden part of the dock, the pilings are ¼" dowels cut into 1¾" lengths. The horizontal planking is ¼" x 1⁄16" stripwood cut into 4½" lengths. The wooden cap at the edge of the concrete is a ¼" square piece of stripwood.

Before staining, I scraped the wood pieces with a hobby saw to create grain and then sprayed them with white primer. I used Minwax American Walnut water-based wood stain on the dock and pilings. On pieces placed near the water's surface, I added a coat of clear gloss Minwax Polycrylic for a wet look, **3-7**.

The rope used to tie the pilings together is pearl cotton no. 5. It comes in a skein and can be found in the embroidery department at any fabric store. You can age its light tan color with an mix of India ink and rubbing

3-7

The dark strip on the bottom of the pilings is prototypical and also helps blend the pilings into the water. The wet sheen comes from the clear gloss Polycrylic. The rope can be aged with India ink and rubbing alcohol.

3-8

The bollards are made from ⅛" scrapbooking snaps on top of ⅛" styrene tubing. The snaps can be found in the scrapbook department of stores like Hobby Lobby or Jo-Ann Fabric. This particular brand is Making Memories.

3-9

The pilings are spaced 1" center to center, and the bollards are 4" center to center. There are two pilings together where the stripwood pieces overlap. Note the HO rail and wheel stop in the background for the gantry crane.

3-10

The wood piling sea wall is made from vertical bead that I found in the wood crafts section of Jo-Ann Fabric.

alcohol. I used a drop of cyanoacrylate adhesive (CA) to attach one end of the rope to the pilings. Then I wrapped it four or five times around the pilings and applied another bit of glue to the remaining end.

The bollards are ⅛" scrapbooking snaps on top of ⅛" styrene tubing, **3-8**. (For you landlubbers out there, bollards are posts used to secure a ship's mooring line.) For the bases, I cut .040" x .250" Evergreen strip styrene into ¼" squares. I used liquid plastic cement to join the ⅛" styrene tubing to the base. The finished bollards are ⅞" high. CA secured the metal snap to the tubing and the bollard to the dock. I sprayed them with Rust-Oleum Dark Bronze Metallic paint.

I began assembly by gluing the ¼" square stripwood cap flush with the deck. The vertical pilings came next followed by the horizontal boards, **3-9**. I used two pilings side by side where the boards overlap. CA was my adhesive of choice since it allowed me to work quickly.

Making the seawalls

I have both a wooden seawall and a metal seawall on the dock. The wood-piling seawall is made from vertical bead, **3-10**, which I found in the wood crafts section of Jo-Ann Fabric. It's a 2" x 3⁄16" x 36" wooden strip. I stained the wall as I did the dock pilings and attached it to the foam with white glue.

The metal seawall is made from pieces of 5⁄16" x ¾" aluminum window screen frame placed vertically side by side, **3-11**. I sprayed them flat black and created the white salt line and weathering with pastel chalks. Attaching the aluminum presented a problem since you can't use solvent-based glue like CA or Walthers Goo on foam. To solve that problem, I used white glue to secure a piece of adhesive-backed mat board sticky side out to the foam. Pins held the mat board in place while the glue dried. Then I stuck the metal pieces to the wall starting at the dock, **3-12**. I also added a drop of CA to each piece for good measure.

3-11

A square-cut screen frame kit makes for an excellent metal seawall. This particular kit (PL-7807) is manufactured by Prime-Line.

3-12

The metal seawall is capped with a ⁵⁄₁₆" square wooden dowel painted to resemble concrete, and the railing is made by Plastruct. I created the salt line (lower right) with pastel chalk.

3-13

This rock lies at the entrance to the harbor. It was the first and the largest rock used. I secured the rock to the glass with Celluclay, which I mixed with black liquid tempera paint to produce the gray color.

3-14

Here I added brown latex paint to the Celluclay to more closely match the rock color. The dark stain along the water's edge is from American Walnut stain coated with Polycrylic, which adds a wet look.

3-15

Applying layers of masking tape over wadded newspaper is an easy way to form the hillside slope going from the right-of-way to the rocks.

3-16

The paint and subsequent bonding solutions stiffen the tape and provide a surprisingly firm surface.

The rocky shoreline

I thought a natural rocky shoreline across the harbor would provide a nice contrast to a rectilinear concrete, brick, and steel industrial area. I didn't think I could get the look I was after from rock castings, so I gathered up the real thing. Fortunately, there's a place along a railroad siding not far from my house that has just the right kind of rock.

I selected relatively flat rocks and broke them apart with a hammer, placing the flattest pieces on top of the glass, **3-13**. I kept adding and subtracting rocks until I found a basic arrangement that I liked. Even so, there were many places that didn't conform to the water's surface. To fix that, I simply slipped tiny chips under the overhang to fill any obvious gaps. The shoreline consists of dozens of rocks, yet you would never know it.

To secure the rocks to the glass, to the foam, and to each other, I used Celluclay as mortar. It's instant papier-mâche, adheres to almost any surface, and has a long working time. To prepare, you simply mix it with water.

Celluclay can be precolored with anything that's water soluble, and I added brown latex paint so it better matched the color of the rocks, **3-14**. Along the bottoms of the rocks, I used a dark walnut stain to blend any discrepancies into the shadows. You'll notice that I use this same technique on anything that sits on top of the glass.

To sculpt a rugged shore between the tracks and the rocks, first create a jagged edge in the foam with a serrated knife. Then stuff newspaper into any gaps between the rocks and foam. Apply 2"-wide masking tape over the paper to rough in the slope from the right-of-way to the rocky shoreline, **3-15**.

Brown latex paint seals the tape and provides a base coat, **3-16**. It also gives you a good idea of how the final slope will look. Don't be afraid to add more paper and tape if necessary. Then paint it again and evaluate. In many cases, you can add ground cover and other scenic textures right over the painted tape. But in order to seamlessly blend the hillside into the rock, I first applied Celluclay to the tape and painted it to match.

Creating realistic scenery is all about smooth transitions from one area to another, **3-17**. Subtle variations in color and texture in an ever-changing pattern add depth to a scene and make it more lifelike. To complete the scene, I added ground cover to the wet paint. The hillside scenery is a combination of Woodland Scenics light green and yellow coarse turf, my own finely sifted Rock Creek Sand, and natural sheet moss, **3-18**. Although I hand-picked the yellow moss from a friend's yard, you can buy moss in bags at Hobby Lobby.

Now, all that remains for a complete harbor scene is the addition of the bascule bridge, which is a whole nother chapter.

3-17

This area of natural geography provides a nice visual contrast to the hard-edged ribbons of steel and the other man-made intrusions on the layout.

3-18

On the rocky hillside, the fisherman gives us a clue to the size and proportion of the rocks. The rocks are covered with moss, sand, and coarse turf.

4-1

Bridging the gap

As it works the Sandy Harbor industrial district, in a scene repeated several times a day, the New York Central 622 trundles across the well-maintained bascule bridge, which is the centerpiece of the harbor.

No harbor scene worth its salt would be complete without some type of bridge, and the Sandy Harbor is no exception. I have always loved the Lionel bascule bridge and decided it would be just the ticket for the harbor entryway, **4-1**. However, I did have one concern—how could I make a beautiful prewar tinplate accessory fit into the detailed, scale hi-rail layout I had in mind? I knew that I could conceal the green base, but painting the bridge structure was out of the question, and the bright yellow shack with the red roof had to go.

4-2

The Decorflex foam retaining walls come two to a package. Don't let the HO tag fool you. These cut stones will fit right into an O scale layout.

4-3

It took no time at all to cut and fit these pieces together. A little spackle fills any gaps, and some stain, chalk, and Polycrylic color the walls.

4-4

In order to hide the binding posts, I fashioned a new deck out of plastic sheet. To get the dimensions, I first made a paper template of the area.

4-5

The wires go through the motor shaft slot in the bridge tender's shack to a terminal strip underneath the layout.

Disguising the base

Concealing the sides of the bridge's base was simple. I used Faller's Decorflex natural-cut stone retaining walls (no. 170804), **4-2**. These 5" x 14" foam sheets cut easily with a hobby knife, and I placed them around the water's edge and in other areas of the layout, **4-3**.

There is one minor drawback in using the retaining walls. They are colored only on the surface, so you can see blue foam in the grooves between the stones. I fixed this by brushing dark gray and brown pastel weathering powders into the mortar joints. I also used these chalks to create the color variation on the shoreline rocks.

I wanted to show that the bottom of the retaining wall was wet. To create a wet look, I darkened a strip of foam with Minwax American Walnut wood stain and then coated it with Minwax clear gloss Polycrylic. These water-based products do not harm the foam.

After coloring the foam, I attached the walls to the base foam with white glue, holding them in place with straight pins while the glue dried. I topped the walls with a concrete cap made from .100" x .250" Evergreen strip styrene. It's colored with Uline tan Maskout spray paint and secured to the foam core with cyanoacrylate adhesive (CA). Because any solvent-based glue will attack foam, I first sealed the foam's edge with white glue.

To finish disguising the base, and to neatly hide the wiring, I covered the base's top with .040"-thick Evergreen styrene sheet (no. 9040), **4-4**. To clear the binding posts, it needed to be ⅝"above the base. The color-coded wires slip through the motor shaft slot in the bridge tender's shack and attach to a terminal strip underneath the layout, **4-5**. I suppose I could have used a more direct route, but the cutout was already there.

Replacing the shack

After removing the tinplate shack by straightening the tabs that hold it to the base, **4-6**, I toyed around with several ideas for its replacement, which needed to be simple and readily available. I looked through my kit stash and decided on using the first story of the Atlas signal tower, **4-7**. The building's brick walls had just the right look, and its width fit perfectly.

Adding the new building was a relatively easy process, but it did require some modification, including a new roof, a new porch, and a little plastic surgery. I also rearranged the walls to give the bridge tender a better view of the harbor. If you've never done any kitbashing before, you might want to check out chapter 8 first.

The first step is to remove the small upper section from the two side walls to make them level, **4-8**. Using a hobby knife, I scored a line on the rear of the

4-6 **The tinplate shack is easily removed by carefully straightening the bottom tabs that anchor it to the bridge. The slot in the building slips over the motor's drive shaft.**

4-7 **One you start looking at a kit for its components, you'll see many possibilities. The brick first floor stood out as a near perfect replacement for the bridge tender's building.**

casting. I made the line, guided by the wall's raised rib, with the back of the knife blade, and then finished the cut with the sharp edge. I also cut a slot in the corresponding side wall, so it could slip over the motor shaft, **4-9**.

The length of the walls needed to be shortened by 7/16". This allows the shack to fit between the binding posts and the raised rib on the platform's base. The walls measure 5 11/16", and I cut them down to 5¼". On the slotted wall, I trimmed the excess from the window end, and on the other wall, from the solid side. You can bevel the cut ends for a smooth corner joint and easier assembly. To finish adjusting the walls, you need to match the height of the taller rear wall with the other three walls.

Moving to the bottom of the building, I created a concrete foundation of .125" x .250" strip styrene for all four walls. Mounting it flush with the back side presents a tiny reveal, or edge, along the front. At the front entrance, I build a porch with stairs (see pages 34-35).

To attach the roof, I added gables to the front and rear walls, **4-10**. Cut from .060"-thick Evergreen sheet styrene, the gables fit behind the tabs at the top of the walls and are flush with the brick. Each gable is 1" high at its peak. I glued V-grooved .100" x .020" sheet styrene on the gables to represent vertical siding. Then I added a cornice that covers the top 2½ rows of bricks at the top of each wall, **4-11**. It is made from .040" x .125" strip styrene.

Before adding the roof, it was easier to paint and weather the building. I sprayed the brick walls with Rust-Oleum rusty metal primer and used Uline tan Maskout on the concrete foundation. All of the door and window casings, cornices, vertical siding, porch, and steps were first given a coat of flat gray primer. After letting them dry overnight, I then sprayed them with Rust-Oleum Deep Forest Green Camouflage.

When the paint dried, I lightly distressed the surfaces with a miniature metal bristle brush. This removed some of the green color to reveal the gray underneath—instant weathering. I used a pencil eraser on the doors to create a slightly different effect. With a fingertip, I applied spackle to the brick surface to simulate mortar. Extra residue was easily removed with a slightly damp paper towel.

The roof is made from .060" sheet styrene and covered with rolled roofing. It measures 1⅞" wide from the peak and has a 5¾" length, which allows for a ¼" overhang from each end of the structure. If you cut a piece of 9" x 12" black construction paper in 1"-wide strips along its 12" length, you'll end up with enough roofing material for this project—and a few others. Start laying your first strip at the bottom. The next strip should overlap the first by about ¼". The third strip straddles the peak and should overlap the strips on both sides. To add a realistic weathered look, slide a piece of gray chalk down the roof.

I vented the kit's exterior sewer pipe through the roof by adding a piece of plastic tubing from my scrapbox. A

4-8 **The small brick sections were removed with a hobby knife to even up the walls. The lower brick wall is used as the slot wall.**

4-9 **The slot is 5/16" wide and 2⅛" from the window end. Shortening the wall from that end allows the shaft to extend through the window opening.**

4-10 **The rear wall (with window) has been cut down to match the height of the other walls. The gable awaits vertical siding and a cornice.**

4-11

The gables now have vertical siding above the cornice. I filled unused holes with spackle, cementing pieces of plastic on the inside as backing for the filler. This should have been done early on, but I was in a hurry.

4-12

Wow! There's no comparison to the original tinplate shack on the bright green base. This shows that you can combine the best of both worlds into one credible scene. Yet, I wasn't totally satisfied.

4-13

Simply by replacing the stone wall with an extended concrete foundation, this version of the bridge tender's shack ties everything together better.

4-14

I removed the stone wall and dug a trench around the base to accept the new foundation. A drywall screw anchors the base to the tabletop.

Berkshire Valley stove pipe was the finishing touch to the bridge tender's shack—or so I thought. Then I placed the completed building over the motor's shaft and onto the base, **4-12**.

Finishing what you start

The bridge was incorporated into the layout, and each disguising element did what it was designed to do: the stone wall naturally masked the sides of the base, and the shack cleverly concealed the motor. But to be honest, I was not completely satisfied with the end result. I just didn't like the way the building sat on top of the wall. There was a disconnect.

The solution was to eliminate the stone wall and extend the building's foundation, **4-13**. That idea didn't occur to me when I started the process. This illustrates how building a hi-rail layout is a dynamic process—even those of us with experience still make it up as we go along. Oh, and that reminds me—I still need to add exterior lights over those doorways…

Making the new foundation

To begin the renovation, I lifted the shack off the bridge's base. Then, after removing the stone wall, I cut a shallow trench in the foam around the bridge's exposed base that would accept the new foundation, **4-14**. With three .080" x .250" strips of styrene, I extended the building's base on the two corresponding walls to cover the exposed corner of the bridge's base, **4-15**. I glued the pieces to the foundation one row at a time. For added stability to the shack's walls, I glued pieces of .125" x .250" strip styrene inside the building, **4-16**. I then sanded the foundation to remove the telltale seams. Next, I sprayed it with gray primer to reveal any remaining joint lines. More sanding, followed by a thin application of body putty, created an even surface for final painting, **4-17**. I then masked off the brick walls and sprayed the foundation with the tan Maskout spray.

Mounting the bascule bridge

In photo **4-14**, you'll notice that the bridge's base is shimmed up with a piece of foam core. This raises the bridge track to match the height of the track throughout the harbor. Since I used foam core to lock the harbor glass in position, this also raised the upper level of the 2" construction foam by ³⁄₁₆". I let

Building a small porch with stairs

I've always liked how a small wooden porch with steps seems to add so much character to a model. The bridge tender's shack seemed like a good choice for a porch. I followed a prototypical construction method that you can follow, using Evergreen styrene and a Grandt Line 45-degree wooden staircase (no. 3533). The illustrations are drawn to 1:48 scale (¼" = 1'). Since the drawings are to scale, you can copy them and use them as templates to get your measurements. (You can copy the templates for your own use but may not distribute them to others.) The deck is a reasonable size for most buildings, but the orientation of the stairway and the number of steps should naturally be configured to suit your particular application.

Frame

The first order of business is to build the deck frame (**Fig. 1**). For the sides, cut two 13/16" pieces from the .040" x .125" styrene. Cut a 1⅜"-long front piece, which spans the two side pieces. The back piece rests between the side pieces. Carefully line up the strip with the illustration, make your mark, and cut to size. An easy way to assemble this frame is to make two L-shaped pieces and then glue them together as a rectangle. To do so, line the pieces up against the inside corner of a metal square. Hold them in position, apply a drop of liquid plastic cement, and let it set up. After everything dries, clean up the edges with a file, if necessary.

Deck

Cut the deck boards from the .040" x .125" styrene. The boards overhang the front by the width of a board, by just a hair on each side, and are flush with the back. Notch the two end boards as indicated in **Fig. 2**. Use a .080" x .080" piece to check your alignment. Carefully line up the first board. Apply liquid plastic cement to the frame—capillary action will draw it under the board. When it's dry, this board will serve as a guide for the other boards. Add the remaining deck boards to the frame one at a time. Before gluing on the last two, check the fit with the corner post and make any final adjustments.

After the deck sets up, paint it using the same two-step painting process as described for the doors and windows (on page 32) but don't paint the underside. When that's done, glue the deck to your wall. Center it with the doorway and butt it right up to the bottom of the threshold. Apply the glue from the bottom.

Posts

Cut the posts from .080" x .080" styrene. The trickiest part of this step is making sure that the posts are perpendicular. Here's what I did. First, I scraped the paint off the posts where

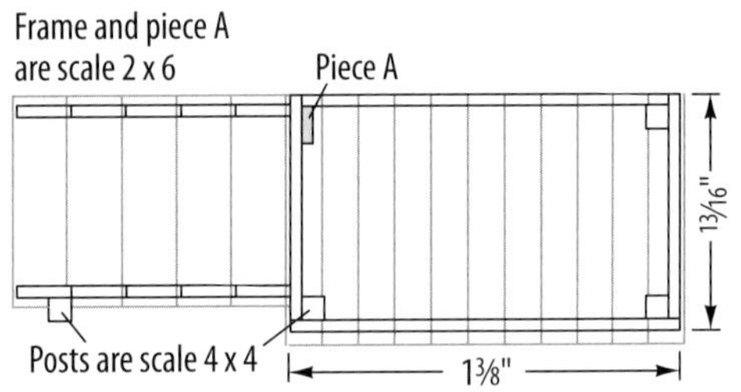

Fig. 1 Frame—top view

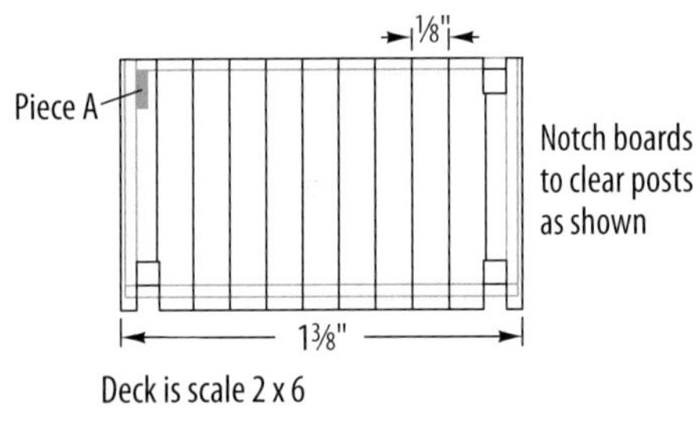

Fig. 2 Deck—top view

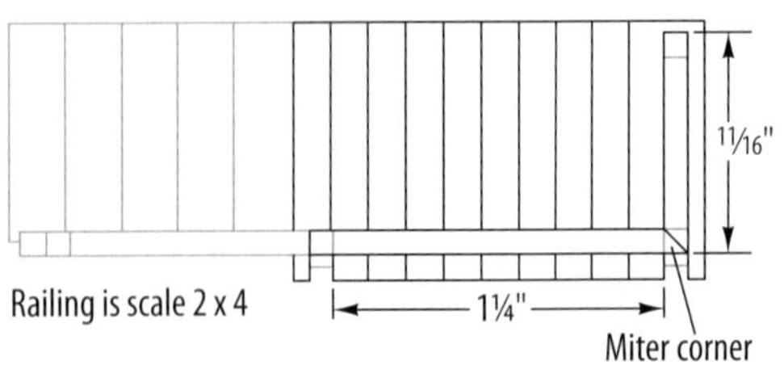

Fig. 3 Porch rail

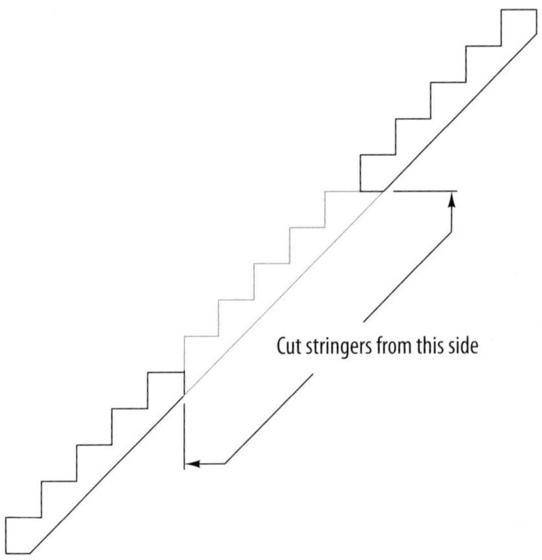

Fig. 4 Stair stringers

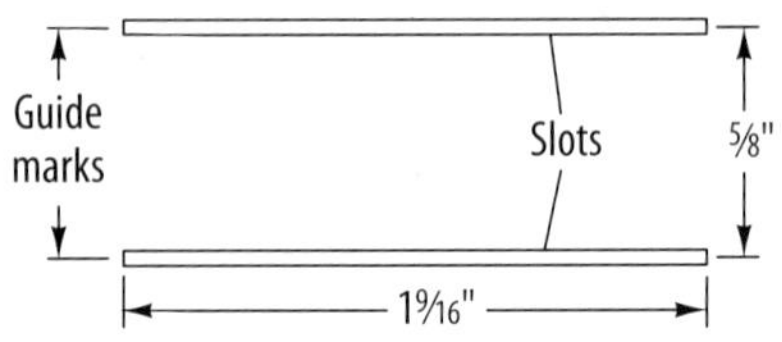

Fig. 5 Stringer template

they would be in contact with the unpainted frame. Then, I inserted the front posts through the holes, letting them rest on the base. Next, I pretty much eyeballed it while holding up a square as a guide. Finally, using a toothpick, I transferred a tiny drop of plastic cement to the frame. Since the cement actually softens the plastic, you have some time to finagle it. I did the same with the shorter rear post.

Railing

Cut the porch rail from the .040" x .080" styrene. The corner angle is 45 degrees (**Fig. 3**). Join them together on your workbench and then glue the railing to the posts. Cut your pieces just a tad longer and file to fit before gluing.

Steps

I cut two 3-step stringers from the single 15-step stringer (**Fig. 4**). The drawing shows five steps, but I only needed three to cover the distance from the sidewalk. Your distance may vary so measure accordingly.

Copy the stringer template in **Fig. 5** and glue it to a piece of foam core. Line up your straightedge with the guide marks and cut in the slots with a sharp hobby knife. Insert the stringers, making sure they're even with the black line and perpendicular to the surface. Run the bottom corner edge of the stringer along the slot to widen it before insertion. Then glue on the treads one at a time. The locater strips on the bottom of the treads go on the inside of the stringers. Let the steps dry thoroughly before removing and then notch out the first two treads to accommodate the bottom post.

This typical wooden porch design is appropriate for any building or era. (Stringer differs from illustration.)

Add the stringer support just below the porch deck frame as shown in **Fig. 6**. You'll need to add a hanger (piece A) as a backing for the left side of the stringer support.

Carefully position the stairway against the stringer support. According to the plan, with the left side of the stairway against the wall, the handrail post should be in line with the porch posts (**Fig. 7**). To check, place a straightedge against the porch posts—the handrail post should fall along the same line. When you're happy with the alignment, secure the stairway to the stringer support with CA. To finish, add the post and the banister.

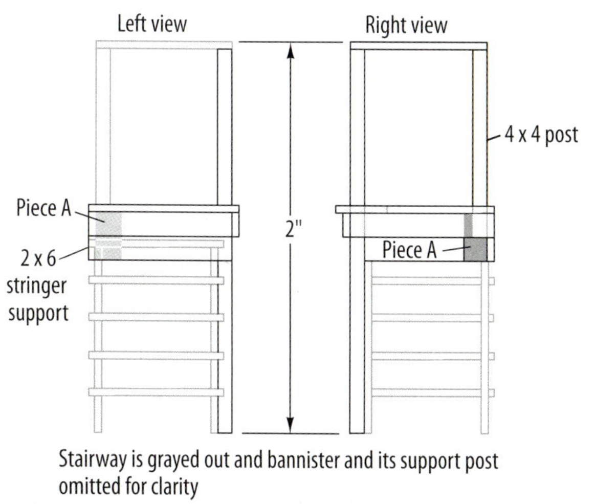

Fig. 6 Porch—left and right views

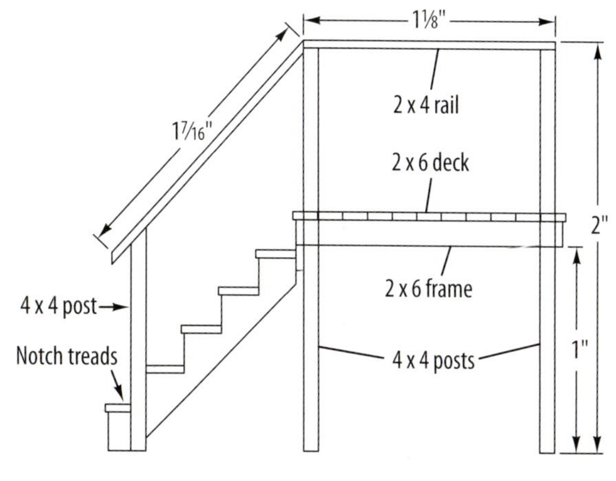

Fig. 7 Porch—side view

4-15

I used three strips of .080" x .250" Evergreen strip styrene to extend the building's foundation.

4-16

Extending the foundation on two sides allows the building to overlap the corner of the bridge's base. Although I added interior support pieces to the walls, there was no practical way to eliminate the slight bow in the slotted wall because of clearance issues with the motor.

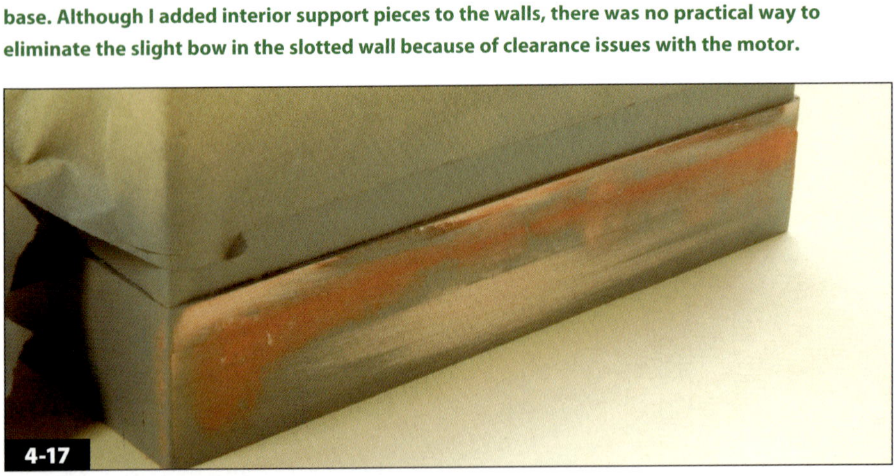

4-17

Masking tape protects the building from overspray. The foundation has been primed, sanded, and puttied. It will be primed again before the final concrete coat is applied.

the bridge-approach track take a natural grade from its branch off a preceding turnout—a distance of almost 3 feet. This rise is imperceptible, both visually and operationally.

Many prewar and postwar bascule bridges suffer from a slightly warped base due to excessive spring tension. Mine was no exception. I corrected this problem by pulling the base down with drywall screws. Since the foam is not solid enough to hold a screw under that much pressure, I simply glued a square wooden peg into a square hole in the foam. This is a good trick for any place where you need a solid screw mount in a piece of foam.

Modifying girder bridges

I didn't want the harbor to feel constricted by a narrow entrance. Strategic bridge placement helped make the entrance seem larger. Because the bascule bridge's abutment juts out into the harbor, it pushes the other end of the bridge that much farther across the waterway, which creates the impression that the bridge spans a greater distance. By combining a girder bridge with the bascule bridge, the space opens up even more and makes the harbor seem bigger than it is. And since I have always liked the look of that prototypical combination, adding a girder bridge was a no-brainer. I also had to add a second girder bridge at the other end of the harbor, and both bridges needed some modifications.

I selected a diecast Lionel girder bridge (no. 314) for the bridge at the harbor entrance. Since it would rest in the water, it needed some supporting concrete piers. I cut two 2" tall, round concrete piers from a 1¾" (outside

4-18

Nothing fancy here. Readily available materials, paint, and a little weathering combine to make realistic concrete piers. It's not the substance, but the treatment that makes the difference.

diameter) cardboard tube, **4-18**, which I found in my junk drawer, but you can substitute 1½" PVC plumbing pipe. Wrapping 2" masking tape around the tube hid the seams. I then added a .030" x .125" styrene strip at the top with CA to represent a concrete sill and capped each pier with .060" sheet styrene. The piers were sprayed with Uline tan Maskout paint to represent aged concrete and then weathered similarly to the other objects sitting in the water. I used Minwax American Walnut stain followed by clear gloss Polycrylic to create the wet sheen along the bottom. To make the watermark, I held the edge of a brown chalk stick against each pier as I rotated it, and then repeated the process with white chalk to add the salt line. The piers are bonded to the glass with CA. Their location was established early on since they actually support the track. The stone bridge abutments were made from the Faller stone retaining walls.

In order to better align the girder bridge with the bascule bridge, and to accommodate two walkways, I had to widen the bridge about ⅝", so I cut the bridge in half lengthwise with a hacksaw and a metal-cutting blade.

The track rests directly on the separated metal base, **4-19**. I added the wooden walkways to provide interest, **4-20**, and they hide the fact that there is no real substructure underneath. The planks are ¹⁄₁₆" x ¼" stripwood weathered with an India ink and alcohol mixture. I extended every fifth tie with a piece of .188" x .250" strip styrene to support the planks. The planks and tie extensions were attached with CA.

I used a two-tone misting technique to color and weather the plate girders. First, spray on a base coat of flat black and let it dry. Then apply the mist by holding the can far enough away so that the paint particles are almost dry upon contact. This builds up a slight texture. Finally, mist it again using Rust-Oleum rusty metal primer. Only this time, spray at a downward angle, so only the edge of your spray hits the lower half of the girders. It's actually very easy to do and quickly produces realistic results, **4-21**, but you might want to practice on a piece of paper until you get a feel for it.

4-19

The track spans the separation in the metal base. It's hard to believe that the concrete piers are made from cardboard tubes, masking tape, and some plastic.

4-20

Although the wide angle of the photo exaggerates the perspective, the near end (right) of the bridge is slightly wider because of the curve leading into it.

4-21

It doesn't get any more realistic than this. This closeup shows what can be done with ordinary spray paint and chalk weathering.

Using two girder bridges to span this outlet adds visual interest and also expands the scene.

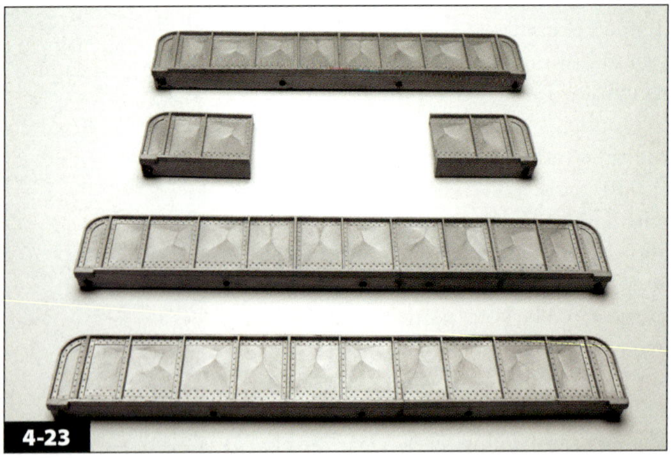

It's very hard to see the seams in the kitbashed spans (between fourth and fifth panels from the left). After they're painted, you'll never know the difference.

The wires for the lift-out section are routed through the tabletop just to the left of the coal pile. The hole will be hidden with a removable pile of ties. Notice that the bridge track sections overlap onto the tabletop instead of being gapped to fit within the lift-out section.

Having a wide outlet on the far end of the harbor also adds to the feeling of a large port. Unfortunately, I could find no commercial bridges wide enough to use on one curve. Ah, but not to worry. The old, reliable girder bridge saved the day once again, **4-22**. I dug into my train stash and came up with three postwar, plastic girder bridges—two Colbers and a Marx. These bridges are direct copies of Lionel's no. 314 girder bridge, so they match the other girder bridge.

The bridge girders are normally 9¾" (eight panels) wide. Because the outlet tapers as it runs under the tracks, I needed to span 24" on the harbor side but only 17" on the other side. After carefully drilling out the rivets to remove the girders from the metal base plate, I cut and spliced them together

The bridge supports are made from Faller's natural cut stone retaining walls. The abutments are glued in position while the center support pier is free-floating. When the bridge is in place, the seam in the glass is covered.

More than anything else, subtle color variations create the scene's realism, so plastic girders can replicate metal, foam panels appear as cut stone, and a sheet of glass reflects water.

Girder bridge design

There are two types of plate girder bridges: deck and through. On a deck-plate girder bridge, the trains run on top of the girders. On a through-plate girder bridge, the trains run through them. Either type may have an open deck or a ballasted deck. When underneath clearance is an issue, through-plate girder bridges are normally used.

Plate girders are I-beams made up from separate structural steel plates, which are welded, bolted, or riveted together to form the vertical web and horizontal flanges of the beam. A popular misconception is that railroads used curved plate girders to support curving track, **1**. Some modelers insist that they've seen curved railroad bridges. The fact is these "curved" bridges use a series of short straight spans to form an arc that, from a distance, do, indeed, appear to form a continuous curve, **2**. The deck itself may be curved, but the support structure is not, **3**.

Today, you will find curved I-beam, box, and tub girder bridge designs being used for highway flyovers and light rail. These designs have become popular during the past 30 years or so. Two of the very first curved steel box girder designs in the United States were built in Massachusetts during the early 1960s. Prior to that, curved girders of any sort didn't exist. And to this day, I'm not aware of any railroad using a curved plate girder bridge.

1

From a distance, this deck girder bridge appears to be curved.

2

Looking from the opposite direction, you still might assume that the girders are curved.

3

Upon closer inspection, you can see that the girders are straight while the deck is curved.

to make a pair of 10-panel and a pair of 7-panel girders.

This is a very easy alteration. To make the 10-panel span, I simply cut one 8-panel girder in half, giving me two 4-panel sections. Then I combined each one with a matching 6-panel section cut from two other girders. I used the rib as the cutting guide, making sure each mating cut was on the appropriate side. Making the splices along the ribs effectively hides the seams, **4-23**. For the 7-panel girders, I just cut out one panel from two of the 8-panel girders.

The bridge deck is made from ¼" plywood covered with foam core. I made this into a lift-out section for cleaning and photographic purposes. Because of that, its track is wired independently, **4-24**. The wires run through a trench cut in the foam core that is covered with masking tape. They're then routed down through the tabletop. Wire nuts tie them into the system, making it easy to unwire when removing the section.

Although the tracks are permanently attached to the deck, I did not cut them to fit within the removable span. Instead, I let the curved track pieces hang over the edges on each end. This way I had a way to anchor the bridge tracks to the tabletop, ensuring a perfect vertical alignment. Drywall screws, placed between the ties, are good enough to secure the overhanging tracks to the underlying foam.

The center stone pier is decorative, functional, and prototypical, **4-25**. The stone walls surround an 18⅝" x 1½" piece of insulation foam. The pier is not permanently attached to the glass as the weight of the bridge holds it in position. The plate girders simply rest on the abutments and are not attached to the deck.

With the bridges in place, the harbor is basically complete, and the scene achieves a realistic appearance, **4-26**. Now we can turn our attention to creating other areas of the layout.

5-1

Will build to suit

When modeling this location, affectionately known as Kate's Crossing, I was influenced by similar areas seen in photos, such as the one in photo 5-2. Notice how the black and white crossing gates, the red fire hydrant, and the blue and purple café curtains add a little pop in a scene painted with subdued earth tones.

As a photographer, I tend to think in pictures, and from the get-go, I had a grand vision for the Sandy Harbor Terminal Ry. But having a mental picture is one thing, actually seeing it through to fruition is something else. I have to admit there were times when I questioned my sanity—as my wife will attest to. But still, the challenge was invigorating.

5-2

This photo and others like it provided the inspiration for the street leading into the heart of the harbor industrial area. *Photo by Matt Herson*

Even though I frequently draw from my imagination and experience, every scene has to start somewhere—be it the leftover impressions from a childhood memory or more recent recollections. More often than not, my inspiration comes from an illustration or a photograph, **5-1**. The development of the harbor area was greatly influenced by photos I studied of New York City's harbor railroads, **5-2**.

Creating a model railroad environment is like putting together a three-dimensional jigsaw puzzle. Sometimes you know exactly where a piece will go, but mostly, you just keep trying various pieces until something fits. Usually, you end up completing sections in different areas and then filling in the gaps. And that's precisely how I tackled this project.

Urban planning

There are four basic areas on the Sandy Harbor: the upper-level manufacturing zone, the harbor-warehouse district, the hillside residential section, and the small industrial block below it. While there is a homogeneous blend, each of these neighborhoods has a particular flavor.

The background cityscape, with its manufacturing area, skirts a downtown that presumably lies just beyond what we can see, **5-3**. This provides the context for the three other neighborhoods and the railroad that runs along the back of the big city. (Creating the cityscape is described in chapter 6.)

The harbor district bustles with activity, **5-4**. Leading into it, you'll see a restaurant, two bars, and a shabby hotel with its own watering hole. The dockside crane and a warehouse are shoehorned into a densely packed industrial district—definitely the other side of the tracks.

The blue-collar, hillside residential neighborhood offers a contrast with its wooden three-story tenements and a row of brick storefronts with overhead apartments. A variety shop, paint store, and a drycleaner make up three local mom-and-pop establishments, **5-5**.

At the bottom of the hill, there is a small industrial pocket along Garfield Avenue, a main drag that runs through the urban sprawl. Another commercial retail pocket is across the street from two railside factories. The hole-in-the-wall Garfield News flanks a much larger nameless brick building. Sandwiched between it and Rob's Radiator Repair is a nondescript, three-story structure with a boarded-up top floor, **5-6**.

These descriptions could fit the neighborhoods of many major metropolitan areas. In the residential neighborhood where I grew up in the 1950s, many buildings contained first-floor businesses with upstairs apartments or were flat-roofed buildings connected to family homes. Within three contiguous blocks, a butcher shop sat on one corner, a soda fountain anchored another corner, and a deli and a gas station were bookends to a row of houses in the middle

5-3 **The background cityscape is made up of kitbashed HO scale buildings. The multiple heights create an interesting skyline.**

5-4 **With a bascule bridge, tugboat, and cranes, the harbor area teems with activity.**

block. Across the street, a hardware store, shoemaker, drycleaner, barber shop, supermarket, variety store, pharmacy, and beauty salon provided all the basics. And within walking distance, there were two taverns, a liquor store, an appliance shop, an egg store, a TV and radio repair shop, another soda fountain, a bakery, a newspaper-magazine-comic book store, and a pizza joint.

Before the days of big box stores, mega malls, and the interstate highway system, almost every neighborhood contained locally owned businesses. To be sure, every city had its downtown with large department stores, banks, and a movie house, but the day-to-day necessities could be found right in your own backyard.

Since many modelers seem to gravitate to the steam-diesel transition era of the 1940s and '50s, it's relatively easy to populate an urban setting. Even if you're into contemporary railroading, most of the old buildings and houses are still around, but many will have changed. The old corner deli now houses a wedding video production company, the supermarket has expanded into the former variety store, and the service station now only does auto repair, the gas pumps having disappeared long ago. To create a realistic city environment, you don't need a degree in urban planning. All you need to do is visit any old section of a city. Everything you need to know is right there. You just have to see it.

Area development

After I laid out the waterfront, I turned my attention to laying the rest of the trackwork, installing the essential wiring, and assembling the components that help establish the urban setting for the Sandy Harbor.

Although the track will rest neatly on the uniform foam surface, I stacked additional pieces of foam board to gain

5-5

The date on the building shows that this is an old neighborhood, and the vehicles indicate that the scene is from the mid-1950s. Check out the understated details that breathe life into this scene. There's an apartment for rent above the paint store. The unused sign bracket above the dry cleaner hints at a previous business. Rolled up awnings with hand cranks provide further evidence of a bygone era.

5-6

A block of commercial buildings similar to this one is a common sight in an urban area. The differing heights, shapes, and colors help these brick structures retain their individuality while adding to the hodgepodge look of the city.

5-7

NYC 622 is about to cross the girder bridge over the Garfield Avenue underpass. This dramatic scenes created on the Sandy Harbor Terminal Ry. is one that often takes place in real life.

elevation and used foam core and ceiling tiles to create natural surroundings for the urban structures and roads. In addition to providing a raised base for the city, which ranges from 8" to 12", the foam sheets also help form the two tunnels that disguise the layout's figure-eight loops.

Building the underpass

Having a street dip down to pass under the right-of-way is typical in real life but seldom seen on layouts. And I knew from the beginning that this was a must-have for the Sandy Harbor. The roadway underpass shows how a 4"-change in height can lay the groundwork for a dramatic city scene, **5-7**. While a flat tabletop has the advantage in simplifying benchwork construction, it is very limiting. But by adding two layers of foam to my tabletop, I was able to cut out a portion of the base to create a descent. This elevated the right-of-way without raising the track.

Since there is seldom enough space to model streets with parking on both sides, I generally use a width of 6" from curb to curb. To that, I add another 2¼" for sidewalks (1" sidewalk and ⅛" curb on each side) for a total of 8¼", which is prototypical for older residential neighborhoods.

Using these measurements, you can lay out all of your streets. But with the underpass, you'll need to allow an additional 3/16" on each side to accommodate the foam core retaining walls. The street is not at a right angle to the edge of the layout or to the track. This means that the girder bridge has to be skewed in order to span the roadway. The plate girders are not even parallel to each other because of the turnout on the bridge. You can often create a more dynamic scene when you don't limit your thinking to a strictly rectangular universe. The prototype doesn't conform to a boxed-in reality and neither should we.

Outline the streets on the foam with masking tape. After marking the foam, remove it and do the cutting away from your tabletop. I used a saber saw with a knife-edge blade. Once that's done, the foam sheets can be glued to each other and to the tabletop with white glue. Next, you can begin installing the retaining walls, streets, sidewalks, and girder bridge.

Concrete retaining walls

For the retaining walls that lined the sides of the underpass, I used 3/16" foam core. I cut the foam core with a hobby knife, making the walls 3/16" shorter than the insulation foam behind them, **5-8**. This provided a solid shelf for a 5/16"-square styrene cap that topped the walls and rested above the scenery base.

With an awl, I scored lines into the retaining walls every 10" to represent joints, being careful not to break through the surface. For an aged-concrete appearance, I sprayed the walls and cap with Uline tan Maskout paint.

By first sealing the edge of the foam core with white glue, I was able to use cyanoacrylate adhesive (CA) to attach the plastic cap to the foam, **5-9**. Since you need an all-purpose glue to join

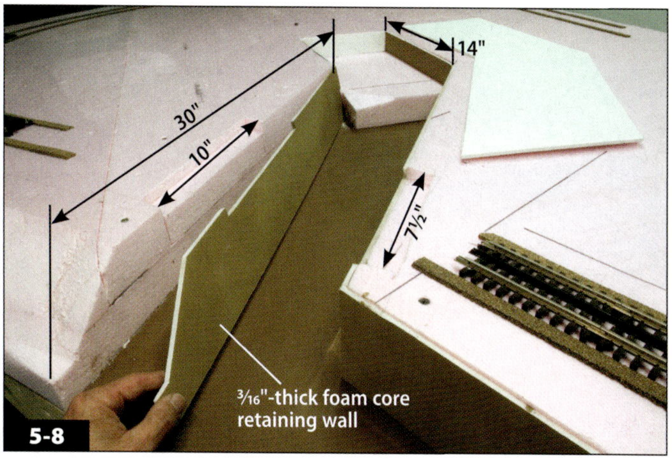

5-8

The white piece of foam core to the right will form the street slope. Note the inset cut into the foam for the girder bridge.

5-9

The cap should be painted before applying it to the top of the walls. (It is shown here unpainted for clarity.)

5-10

The foam core street has been primed with dark gray spray paint. Note the gentle vertical curve of the sidewalk on the left compared to the street.

5-11

There's nothing fancy or exotic here. The evolution of the sidewalk started with a ⅛" thick yardstick from Ace Hardware.

plastic to foam, CA is a good choice here. I used white glue to bond the foam core to the insulation.

Streets and sidewalks

I also used foam core as a base for the streets. Spraying it with dark gray primer undercoats and seals it, **5-10**. After the paint dries, attach the sidewalks with white glue.

The sidewalks are made out of cheap yardsticks, **5-11**. As luck would have it, a typical yardstick is 1⅛" wide by ⅛" thick—a perfect size for a 4-foot-wide sidewalk with a 6" curb. The markings on the yardstick usually aren't a problem after being painted. You should barely be able to feel the lines and numbers, if at all.

Spray the yardstick with any white primer, making sure none of the lettering bleeds through the paint. Scribe a ⅛" curb line and 1" joint lines with the back of a hobby knife. Spray the yardstick again with an uneven coat of gray primer, letting some white show through here and there. Then lightly mist it with Uline tan Maskout paint. The idea is to always let the underlying colors affect the top color.

Here's something else to consider: I've used three dissimilar materials to represent concrete—wood, foam core, and plastic. Each one has a smooth, but slightly different, surface texture, and yet their final appearance belies their origin. The concreteness has to do more with color and how it was applied. The same principle applies to streets. It's the overall treatment that allows us to see a material as asphalt and not as its underlying substance. Use a few well-placed details and the mind fills in the rest. If the color and the weathering are correct, it doesn't matter if streets and sidewalks are made out of plastic, wood, foam, or another material.

5-12

By adding black liquid tempera paint to the water putty when mixing it, you'll get a medium gray color that is well suited for roads.

5-13 A thin layer of water putty covers the street. I also used some to smooth out the abrupt change in elevation. The mottled color comes from applying two coats from different mixtures. Note the grate in place.

5-14 I used ½" plywood to span the gap. This will become a through plate-girder bridge with a ballasted deck. The track will run directly on top of the plywood.

5-15 The foam pieces are removable. Another layer of foam will sit on top of this, covering the tracks. The cover pieces will be glued to the wing walls but not to the center support section. The covered tracks will be accessible from the rear.

5-16 The first level of the terracing uses two stacked ceiling tiles. Notice the varying heights and also how the street runs up the hill at an angle to the edge of the layout. It will disappear in a tunnel under the city. I also slightly narrowed the street as it goes back, which forces the perspective.

With the sidewalks firmly in place, use a 6" drywall knife to spread a thin layer of Durham's Water Putty over the entire roadway to create a uniform surface. The putty covers the seams, smooths out transitions between foam core sections, and provides an overall weathered appearance.

Durham's Water Putty is a cream-colored powder that you can find at building centers and hardware stores. When mixed with water, it sets up harder than plaster and is perfectly suited for this application. To tint the putty, you can mix it with any water-based paint or stain, **5-12**. To give it a grayish color, I added black liquid tempera paint.

Add the coloring a little at a time until you get a medium gray. Don't worry if the color is not uniform within a batch or even between batches. Irregularity in the coloring only adds to the weathering effect.

I suggest starting with about a cup of Durham's. Mix it with enough water to get an easily spreadable consistency. Don't try to cover all of your streets with one batch, **5-13**. If you need to, you can certainly mix up more putty. After about 20 minutes, the putty has the consistency of hard soap, which makes it very easy to shave, cut, or carve. I often use a putty knife or a single-edge razor blade to scrape it smooth, if necessary. But I don't try to get a perfectly flat, even surface. If there are any voids or irregularities, I treat them as potholes, cracks, or patches.

Although you can do it after the putty completely hardens, adding street details such as manhole covers and sewer grates is easily done at this point. Simply place a manhole or grate in position, outline it, and then cut through the putty into the foam core. Remove just enough foam core so the cover is flush with the surface of the street. I usu-

5-17

Notice the staggered positioning of the buildings. Even at this rough-in stage, differing levels, various angles, and a variety of materials (concrete, brick, stone, metal, and wood) create a lot of visual interest.

5-18

The ramp that provides vehicle access to the harbor bisects the retaining walls to create different shapes. The parallel lines (center) mark the path of the street.

5-19

The green part of the street is a thin flexible piece of insulation foam, which makes a smooth transition from the ramp to level ground.

5-20

In this industrial area, the street crosses two tracks including a switch. The street tapers at the back as it nears three lower-level backdrop buildings.

ally paint the cutout area dark gray or black. You can patch the area around the cover or sewer grates with more putty if needed.

Look at any well-trafficked street and you'll see lighter colored asphalt where the wheels travel. You can add light streaks to a dark road or dark streaks to a lighter-colored surface. On my roads, I added dark streaks by sliding dark gray pastel chalk along the roadway and blending it in with my finger. To add lighter streaks, use a medium or light gray chalk.

I then used a Prismacolor charcoal pencil to draw on white center lines, but you can use any charcoal or chalk-type pencil. If the lines appear too clean, just dirty them up with some gray chalk.

I also tried using decal striping, but it didn't stick very well and looked too bright. To tone down the striping, I had to spray it with clear matte spray and apply some chalk.

To complete the streets, I add what I call "street schmutz." You know…that very fine, gritty, gray material that collects along curbs, around corners, by driveways, and in potholes. Without it, model streets look much too clean. Ashes from an outdoor grill make great street schmutz.

Girder bridge

A simple piece of ½" plywood forms the deck for the railroad bridge, **5-14**. I made the deck wider at one end (10") than the other (7½") to accommodate the turnout that leads into a siding by Universal Supply. The girder bridge sections were salvaged from a Lionel bridge. I cut the metal base plate lengthwise, and it provided added support for the plywood. (See pages 36-39 for more on modifying girder bridges.)

A roadblock

So now, after installing the remaining trackwork, my next step was to situate

5-21

The engineer blows the horn, and everyone stops to watch New York Central's Empire State Express as it crosses Garfield Avenue over a curved, wooden grade crossing.

two tunnels in the center of the layout. Once I was satisfied that there were no clearance issues, I marked their positions with a black marker. First, I proceeded to build the middle upper level support section, **5-15**, and then I added wings that would cover most of the track along the rear of the layout. At that point, I hit a roadblock on how to seamlessly integrate the two levels. I puzzled over this for some time and finally decided to leave it alone and work on something else.

Hillside neighborhood

I had always envisioned tenements along the stretch of tracks between the tunnel and the girder bridge over the street. And I knew with a little kitbashing that IHC Victorian Row Houses would make credible models. Once I had finished the first one and set it in the space, it hit me—these tenements needed to be stair-stepped up a hillside just like in San Francisco. Bingo! Now, I knew how to connect the two levels, **5-16**.

The landscaping followed a logical path. Narrow hillside properties dictated the use of retaining walls and fences. The right-of-way cuts through the hill on a narrow shelf, and it required retaining walls, which by necessity, must be more substantial. And so it went—the puzzle pieces were falling into place.

The houses in this hillside neighborhood are plotted neither parallel to the street in front nor to the tracks behind. And they're staggered horizontally as well as vertically, which in addition to being prototypical, lends considerable visual interest, **5-17**.

Warehouse district

Laying out the streets is one of the first steps in creating a scene. This goes hand in hand with building placement. At this stage, it's very easy to see what will fit. So what comes first—the street or the buildings? That's like the chicken-and-egg question. The answer is both. All buildings need some sort of public access, and a street is a good place to start.

After my "ah-ha" moment with the hillside terrace, the idea of a street ramping down into the harbor warehouse district was a natural, **5-18**. After all, what better way is there to get goods from a warehouse to the city and back again? Because of the various angles involved in its creation it was easier to build the ramp as a separate module. This piece is more than 8 feet long, **5-19**. Just as I did elsewhere, I used pink foam to create the basic shapes. Again, I used foam core as the street base.

In old industrial areas, streets and tracks intersect everywhere, and I wanted to capture that same look. By arranging the scene diagonally, rather than parallel or at right angles to the front of the tabletop, I created a longer street with greater visual impact, **5-20**. I also tapered the street ever so slightly towards the rear to exaggerate the perspective. White glue holds the foam core in place. Using 3⁄16" foam core for the street base raises its surface almost level with the ties.

Because of the crowded nature of this area, I needed to replace the switch machines on the Atlas O switches. Instead, I opted to use manually oper-

Manual ground throws

1 Manually operated hand throws put model railroaders close to the action, especially when using walk-around throttles.

2 The tie extensions don't have to be glued to the switch ties, but they do need to be solid.

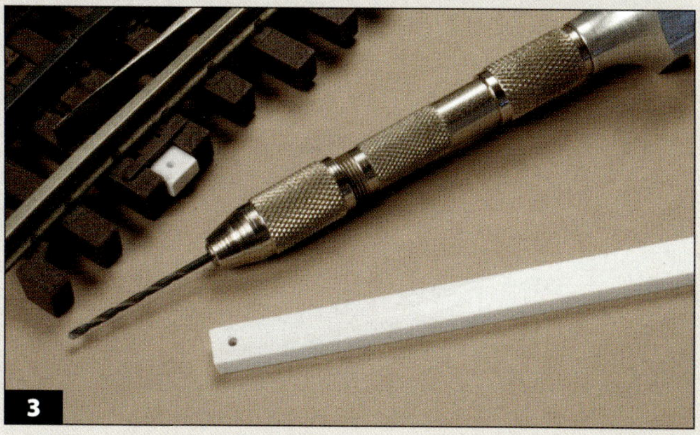

3 It's easiest to first drill the hole in the styrene strip and then cut off the ¼" piece to add to the throwbar.

4 It is critical that the throw bar is accurately positioned to get an equal throw in each direction.

It's very easy to convert an Atlas turnout to manual ground-throw operation, **1**. It can be completed in a few simple steps.

First, extend the switch ties on each side of the throw bar by 1". I mounted 3⁄16" x ⅛" basswood on N scale cork because that is what I had, **2**. You could also use 3⁄16" x ½" stripwood without the cork. If using cork, first attach the cork with white glue. When it sets up, glue the ties to the cork.

Next, add a filler piece to the throw bar to accept the pin from the ground throw. Use a no. 54 drill bit in a pin vise to drill a hole ⅛" from the end of a piece of .125" x .250" strip styrene, **3**. Cut off a ¼" section to situate the hole in the middle. Glue the filler piece to the throw bar with CA.

Center the points between the rails. I used pieces of N scale cork as spacers to keep the points in place, **4**. With the ground throw in the halfway, or vertical, position, insert its pin into the filler piece and mark its position.

Remove the spacers. Hold the ground throw in place and gently move its lever back and forth. The switch points should seat firmly in each direction. Adjust the ground throws if necessary. When you're satisfied with the switch's operation, glue the ground throw to the ties. Walthers Goo works well.

When ballasting, make sure the ballast is clear of the throw bar and well below the rails, so it doesn't interfere with any moving parts.

ated Caboose Industry ground throws (no. 208S.) In fact, I used these everywhere except on the switch behind Carp Machinery, which provides a perfect view block for a street that goes nowhere.

Crossing over

Once I had the streets mapped out, I added the railroad crossings. Putting these in place before topcoating the foam core makes it easier to get a smooth transition from street to crossing.

We've all driven over railroad crossings, but many people pay little attention to them, unless it's a bumpy ride. If you look closely at how they're constructed, you'll see that today's grade crossings are made from many different materials including wood, gravel, concrete, asphalt, rubber, and steel grates. Wooden crossings are still the most common and would be appropriate for any era. Once you understand how they're built, making a realistic wooden crossing is easy, **5-21**.

Crossing mechanics

Grade crossing mechanics are simple. Commonly, wooden grade crossings are made from standard 8"-wide by 8-foot-long railroad ties that are spiked directly to the track ties. In a typical crossing, you'll find six ties placed side by side between the rails and two ties positioned outside of each rail, **5-22**. In places where the track curves or crosses the street at an angle, the ties are usually staggered to match, **5-23**.

This is a typical wooden grade crossing. There are two ties outside each rail and six ties between the rails. Each row of four ties spans 32 feet.

The ties are staggered if the track either curves or crosses the street at an angle. In this case, it does both.

A dome-head drive spike is one you can duplicate on your layout with a sequin pin.

A square-head spike (with washer) is driven into a wooden tie at a crossing.

The width of the roadway determines the length of the crossing. A typical two-lane road with sidewalks and room for parking on both side is about 40 feet, and a corresponding crossing would need a length of five ties placed end to end. Seldom do we have that much real estate on our pikes, so I generally go with a scale 32-foot-wide roadway (including sidewalks), which translates to a crossing four ties long.

To hold the ties in place, real railroads use either square-head or dome-head drive spikes, **5-24**, and the square-head spikes may or may not be recessed into the tie, **5-25**. Usually, three spikes are set into each tie—one in the middle and one about 12" from each end.

When the ties are positioned, the outside ties don't actually touch the rails—there's usually about a 1½" gap. And inside each rail, there's a 3" gap, or flangeway, to accommodate a car's wheel flanges.

Getting started

Now that you know the mechanics of a grade crossing, you can get started with building a grade crossing. A crossing is made from two different sizes of basswood strips, which are needed to provide the necessary ⅛" flangeway. For each 32-scale-foot crossing, you'll need three 12" lengths of ⅛" x ⅛" and four 12" lengths of 5⁄32" x 3⁄16" basswood.

The 5⁄32" stripwood scales to 7½" wide, which is very close to the prototype width of 8". This slightly smaller width conveniently allows for the track's center rail. The 3⁄16" depth brings the height to just below the top of the rails.

The ⅛" x ⅛" strips abut the outside of the outer rails and also go on both sides of the center rail. These smaller strips are needed because of the design of the track, **5-26**.

Because the ⅛" strip doesn't completely cover the tie plate, the adjacent row of 5⁄32" x 3⁄16" ties need to have a beveled edge in order to sit flush on the trackbed, **5-27**. It may be easier to bevel these edges with a few swipes of a small file or sanding pad prior to cutting the ties.

Cutting ties

The first step is cutting the wood strips into 2" ties (8 scale feet). For this task, there are two methods that make short work of cutting numerous pieces of identically sized stripwood.

Using a razor saw and a miter box with a stopping block simplifies the process because you only have to accurately measure the first piece, **5-28**. After cutting the first tie, clean the cut end with a few licks of a file, and then use that tie to position the stop. For subsequent ties, simply slide the stripwood up to the stop and cut.

A Northwest Short Line chopper also makes it easy to cut a pile of identical

5-26 This cross section of Atlas O track shows how the ties fit together. The ties adjacent to the rails sit directly on the spikes. The beveled bottom corner on the adjoining ties allows them to clear the edge of the tie plate.

5-27 This closeup shows how the ⅛" x ⅛" ties rest on the Atlas tie plates and the adjacent 5/32" x 3/16" ties sit on the plastic ties.

5-28 The clamp holds the stopping block in the miter box. Once it is in place, you can easily cut many identical pieces.

5-29 A Northwest Short Line chopper cuts stripwood and styrene. It includes guides for both straight cuts and angle cuts.

5-30 Make sure the ⅛" x ⅛" ties fit snugly against the rails. This is doubly important for the center rail. Glue the ties down in rows, one long strip at a time. Notice how the tie plate peeks out from under the wood.

5-31 Allow for a ⅛" flangeway along the inside of the outer rails. You can test the flangeway by rolling a boxcar through the crossing.

Raising up the building bases to street level also gives some relief to the flat scenery base. The railroad crossings should be in place before finishing the streets.

I used water putty to transition cobblestones to pavement. At this stage, basic ground cover has been added.

The blacktop patches show how an India ink-alcohol wash, gray chalk, and street schmutz give a finished look to the cobblestone street at the grade crossing.

ties, **5-29**. The best way to cut the ties is to cut about one-quarter of the way through on each side. It does go quickly, and you'll end up with accurate right-angle cuts. Although it's tempting, don't try to cut the ties with one chop. The thickness of the wood will deflect the razor blade and cause it to cut at a slant.

After you've cut all the ties, you'll want to stain them before assembling the crossing. For a stain, I mixed one drop of black India ink, one tablespoon of brown drawing ink (available on my Web site or at art supply stores), and one tablespoon of regular rubbing alcohol. This mixture yields an excellent brownish gray color similar to that of a typical weathered wood crossing. Drop the ties into a container of your stain, swish them around a bit, and then remove them for drying.

Start the assembly by gluing the ⅛" ties adjacent to the both sides of the center rail and outside the outer rails, **5-30**. For modeling purposes, the small gap between the outside ties and the rail can be ignored. I used a bit of Walthers Goo along the bottom of the rail to bond the wood to the rail and to the plastic tie plates. You don't need much—a little dab is enough.

A small plastic glue tip on the tube helps put the glue where you need it. Also, it's not necessary to apply Goo to both pieces—we're not looking for strength.

At this point, I did a test fit with the 5⁄32" x 3⁄16" ties. This gave me a chance to square everything up prior to gluing down the remaining ties. Remember to allow for an ⅛" (6" scale) flangeway along the inside of the rails for the wheels, **5-31**. It's also a good idea to roll a railcar back and forth through the crossing to make sure the wheels roll freely.

If everything fits properly, remove the loose ties and then begin gluing them in place. Starting at one end, place a spot of Goo on three or four plastic track ties and then press a wooden tie into position. Repeat this process to complete one row at a time.

To detail the ties, you can add drive spikes. For square-head drive spikes, O scale square bolts and washers by Tichy Train Group (no. 8035) work well. For dome-head spikes, I use ½" sequin pins

5-35

The finished scene of Kate's Crossing, while not an exact reproduction of the prototype shown in photo 5-2, was clearly inspired by it.

5-36

The team track area includes a cobblestone street and a freight dock from one of my model railroading craftsman kits. I kitbashed the gantry crane from Plasticville signal bridge supports and Atlas HO girders, and I scratchbuilt the housing for the crane motor.

5-37

Two layers of foam core bring the surrounding scenery base to rail height in the team track area. Using one layer is an easy way to bury the ties in multiple yard tracks.

GarGraves crossing

If you need to add a crossing to GarGraves track, the process is similar to that for Atlas O, with just a few differences. Since the rails are tubular, you will need some basswood with different dimensions. In addition to four 12" lengths of 5⁄32" x 3⁄16", you will also need three 12" lengths of 5⁄32" x 5⁄32" and three 12" lengths of 1⁄32" x 3⁄32", which are used as shims. The 5⁄32" x 5⁄32" ties abut the rails, and the 5⁄32" x 3⁄16" ties fit outside the others.

Cut the ties as described on pages 50-52. But before cutting the 5⁄32" x 5⁄32" stripwood, use a file or sanding pad to bevel the edge along one side. This prevents the bottom inside corner of the tie from riding up on the foot of the rail and keeps it level with the adjacent ties. Since the 1⁄32" x 3⁄32" shims will be covered, they don't need to be cut into sections. They simply need to span the width of the grade crossing—in this case, 8" (32 scale feet).

To assemble, first snugly glue the shims on each side of the center rail and outside the outer rails as shown. Because you're bonding wood to wood, white glue is a good choice. I found it easier to coat the shims with white glue rather than applying glue to the track ties.

Check the fit of the ties and then glue the 5⁄32" x 5⁄32" ties to the shims, adjacent to the center and outside rails. Remember to place the beveled edge along the base of the rail. Press the ties into position and remove any excess glue with a toothpick. Let those ties set up before adding the 5⁄32" x 3⁄16" ties. While you're waiting for the glue to dry, you can temporarily position the remaining ties before gluing them in place.

Uses shims with GarGraves track to keep the adjacent ties level with the rails. Pins hold the shims against the rail until the glue sets.

5-38

The transition from blacktop to cobblestones between the tracks is hard to detect. Note the areas of broken pavement around the posts.

since their heads are close in scale to the 2¾" head diameter of real spikes. Sequin pins are very small pins used for appliqué and other decorative needlecrafts. They can be found in the sewing department of a store like Jo-Ann Fabric.

Once you get started, the process goes fast. In one evening, you can easily add several realistic grade crossings to your layout.

Finishing up

With the railroad crossings in place, I gave some of the streets a cobblestone surface using gray Plastruct HO scale cement block sheets (no. 91620). I used spray glue to attach the sheets to the foam core, but rubber cement or contact cement works equally well. I added more foam core to raise the building bases up to the street level, **5-32**. I used a hobby knife to carve beveled, irregularly shaped edges into the foam core to help blend it into the surrounding scenery. The masking tape further softens the transition from beveled edge to the layout surface.

I used Durham's Water Putty to transition areas from cobblestone to blacktop, **5-33**. Then, using an India ink and alcohol weathering solution (one tablespoon of black India ink to one pint of rubbing alcohol), I applied dark stains to the cobblestones. Ultimately, I brushed the solution over the entire street. After it dried, I took a slightly damp paper towel and randomly wiped the street to remove some of the stain from the top surface of the raised bricks. This creates realistic tonal variations on the street, which I weathered with a variety of gray chalks, **5-34**.

After the sidewalks were completed, I put down a base layer of scenery. It's composed of a mixture of Brennan's fine and coarse Natural Earth, Rock Creek Sand, and Superior Sand. To complete, I added some Woodland Scenics weeds and grasses, and everything came together in the finished scene, **5-35**.

Team tracks

Many cities had team tracks to service industries that were not located by a siding. The term *team tracks* predates the development of the automobile. At that time, freight was off-loaded directly from boxcars into wooden wagons pulled by teams of horses. These railroad sidings came to be known as team tracks.

Lumber, grain, produce, appliances, and machinery are just some of the goods that might be shipped to or from this simple but vital area, **5-36**. Up through the 1950s, they were fairly common, but today, team tracks and wooden loading docks are hard to find.

Although this site features a cobblestone street, the same idea can be utilized to bury the ties on sidings or in railroad yards. First, I used two layers of foam core to bring the surrounding ground level up to rail height, **5-37**. These pieces butt right up to the ties. I weathered the cobblestones as described earlier. Here, Durham's Water Putty was used to smooth out the change in elevation from the black top to the cobblestones, **5-38**. I beveled the curving edge of the foam core to blend it into the right of way. The posts along the perimeter are ⅛" x ⅛" stripwood spaced 1" apart. A kitbashed gantry crane and wooden loading dock complete the scene.

It took awhile, but the puzzle pieces of the layout's four areas finally fit together in a way that matched my grand vision—almost. The one big piece that I needed to add yet was the cityscape.

6-1

Rising to new heights

The big city bustles with activity in this scene on the Sandy Harbor Terminal Ry. The concept of forced perspective is shown by the use of HO buildings in the background and O scale buildings in the foreground.

I grew up in the shadow of Manhattan, so when I think of a big city, I see brick, steel, concrete, cobblestone, asphalt, and all the little details that add atmosphere such as water tanks, smokestacks, chain link fences, statues, piles of rubble, empty lots, and the list goes on. Although it seems like a daunting task, re-creating this environment on an 8 x 12-foot layout can be achieved through the magic of selective compression and forced perspective, **6-1**.

6-2

This New York harbor scene was a model for the dock and freight house on the Sandy Harbor. *Photo by Allan Roberts*

Selective compression

Accurately reducing a city block, a small industrial complex, or even a warehouse to 1:48 scale would take up an enormous amount of space. However, the key to all of this is keeping in mind that you're creating an illusion. Just as a good movie or novel pulls you in to its fictional reality, allowing you to suspend your disbelief, so should a layout. We're not miniaturizing real life, only capturing its essence. Don't confuse selective compression with building to a smaller scale. They're not the same thing.

For example, a prototypical New York harbor dock with a freight house is at least a dozen boxcars long, **6-2**, which translates to 11 actual feet in O scale. But on the Sandy Harbor, I reduced the dock to less than 3 feet, and the freight house holds two boxcars. The harbor itself is only 8 feet long and about 30" across at its widest point. Is it an exact scale reproduction? Not by a long shot. And yet, I've created a believable scene because I've selectively compressed the main features that shout big-city harbor, **6-3**. It is still 1:48 scale, yet nothing seems out of place because, relative to each other, everything appears to fit. Even the Lionel crane looks perfectly natural in this setting.

6-3

I compressed the dock and freight house, but they still convey the sense of a big-city scene.

Forced perspective

Not long ago, one of my train buddies stopped by to see the layout. After walking around and looking at it, he commented that I had treated each side of the layout as if it were the front. I hadn't consciously thought of that when I designed the layout, but he did have a point. No matter from where you view the Sandy Harbor, you're presented with a visually interesting perspective. And that's where forced perspective comes in.

What is forced perspective? It's using the concept that the farther away an object is, the smaller it appears. This idea is readily employed when it comes to creating mountain scenery as is so masterfully executed on Dave Jacobs' layout, **6-4**. From the lodgepole pines in the foreground to the distant hazy peaks, the scene carries us from one mountain range to another in a space of about 8 feet. Forced perspective applies equally well to an urban landscape.

On an O scale layout, by using HO scale (1:87), or approximately half-scale, buildings in the background, those background buildings appear to be twice as far away, making the layout seem much bigger than it really is. Playing with the relative size of foreground and background objects is an old Hollywood trick that filmmakers have used for years. Creating this illusion for a movie relies on carefully controlled sight lines. But on a model railroad that can be viewed up close and personal from many different viewpoints, you don't always have that option. Once you get the hang of forced perspective, you'll be able to use it to expand your layout's horizons. No one ever notices the change in scale on the Sandy Harbor unless I point it out, and even then, it's not obvious.

Here are some general guidelines when using forced perspective on your layout. If necessary, restrict sight lines by using view blocks. A view block can be a a single building, **6-5**, or a row of buildings, **6-6**. In fact, any object that keeps viewers from seeing what you don't want them to see can be used.

Keep a buffer between any HO scale buildings and your trains. A buffer can be an O scale building, a roadway, a high retaining wall, or even a hill, **6-7**. Creating physical separation keeps you from noticing the difference in scale.

Background buildings should rise above those in the foreground. Sizes are relative. You can use small O scale buildings in front of large HO scale buildings, **6-8**. Where background and foreground buildings are in close proximity, try to match up overall window sizes and avoid doorways. Factory windows can be almost any size, but an HO scale door is a dead giveaway to revealing its scale.

6-4

This scene on Dave Jacobs' layout, which appears to cover a vast distance, is an excellent example of forced perspective. Notice how the trees progressively get smaller from front to back.

Creating a cityscape

The cityscape is perhaps the single most important element in establishing the atmosphere for the Sandy Harbor. In order to capture the big-city feel that I was after, I knew that a background of building flats simply wasn't going to do it.

Instead, I relied on a series of visual tricks to create an overall impression that transcends any one element. First and foremost, the use of HO scale buildings, besides forcing the perspective, allowed me to add many more structures in the available space (selective compression). And by using three-dimensional structures, depth is added to the scene. Juxtaposing the buildings' heights and sizes emphasizes their differences, which further enhances the mixture. Placing a few buildings behind the front elevation alludes to others behind them and creates added dimension, **6-9**. And finally, to give the cityscape greater depth, I staggered the buildings to accentuate their dimension. The uneven skyline gradually climbs to an apex in the dense city center, drawing you into the layout. This is truly an instance where the whole is much greater than the sum of its parts.

If you look at the stair-stepped hillside tenements, they also guide you to

6-5

Here you can see what Carp Machinery (center) is hiding. Through careful positioning, it conceals how the track unrealistically tunnels right behind the false front buildings.

6-6

This row of buildings only allows you to see this tunnel from one angle. The buildings also conceal the end of the layout's upper level from any other angle.

the cityscape's summit. These buildings are, at once, both a background for the trains and an essential part of the layout, and they take the background to another level, **6-10**. All too often, in our quest to fill as much space as possible with track, the background areas, if any, are relegated to a flat line of building facades in front of a printed backdrop.

A dozen different HO scale buildings spanning more than 8 feet went into making the upper level cityscape, **6-11**. The majority are kits from Walthers Cornerstone Series, two are Heljan brewery buildings, and two are from City Classics. With a few exceptions, each structure comes from a single kit that was kitbashed in some fashion. For example, I freely substituted foam core walls for kit walls where they wouldn't be seen. I then used the extra kit walls to expand the structure either horizontally or vertically. Chapter 8 explains how I kitbashed many of these buildings.

You may be wondering if it wouldn't be easier to just use all O scale buildings. Well, the answer is maybe yes and maybe no. It really depends upon the impression you're trying to create. In this case, I wanted to imbue the railroad with the industrialized East Coast atmosphere that colors my childhood memories. To that end—a sprawling jagged skyline dotted with water towers and punctuated with those ever-present smokestacks—would be impossible to achieve with O scale buildings in the same space.

Let's take a tour of the cityscape from left to right. The left section of the cityscape is the tallest and most dense, **6-12**. I turned a Walthers flour mill (933-3026) into Adam Metal Supply, an abandoned factory, and expanded its footprint. Eventually, I'll add a for-sale sign to the building. The Walthers three-story REA transfer building (933-3095) is now a five-story structure, Andrew Roger Manufacturing. By setting this building on a 6" hidden riser and concealing the first floor behind Adam Metal Supply, it appears to be much taller. The narrow, five-story City Classics Ohio Street building (195-106) looks twice as tall because it's resting on a 9" riser with the rear of the building facing out. This is the tallest building within this section, and it nicely fills an open space behind the warehouse. I created TSB Industries' six-story clothing factory from a three-story Walthers Front Street warehouse (933-3069) by stacking the front, back, and side walls. Perched on a hidden 9" riser, a Heljan

6-7

The distance between the center rail and the façade of the Alcoa building is only 14". The high retaining wall, the hillside, the guardrails, and the angled roadway provide relief and visual separation between the full-scale trains and the half-scale buildings.

6-8

The three ground-level buildings are small O scale structures, and the two background buildings are large HO scale factories. You can't see any difference in scale between the buildings, so the illusion of forced perspective works.

6-9

From behind the layout, you see how the background buildings sit on foam risers. A 9"-wide shelf extension allowed me to stack additional buildings behind the cityscape for added depth and provided a place for the lower level background facades on the far corner.

6-10

When seen from any other vantage point, the large HO factory (at left) is a background building. But from this angle, it is viewed with O scale tenements. The tenement windows are big even for O scale, so I had to find an HO building with windows that would not give away its scale.

You can readily see how all the buildings fit together in the this panoramic view of the Sandy Harbor's background cityscape.

brewery building (322-807) appears much taller than its original three stories. Much more of it shows when viewed from the right. Remember, many of these buildings are viewable from more than one angle.

Together, the structures in this section comprise the summit. The taller second-tier buildings serve as a foil to the buildings in front of them. Color, too, plays an important role in providing contrast. The various shapes and sizes create additional visual interest. The water towers add further dimension to what would otherwise be a series of flat roofs against the skyline.

The left center section is dominated by the Aluminum Company of America, **6-13**. It's a stair-stepped conglomeration of buildings that provides a visual transition between two different levels. Having the Alcoa name in two places ties the buildings together, helping us recognize it as a complex. The lower section juts out at an angle from the wall above it. An overhead view would reveal a wedge shaped roof between them. Identical to the Ohio Street building, a City Classics Baum Blvd. building (195-105) sits to the left and behind the warehouse. Barely visible from this view, it functions as a view block and reinforces the perception that there are other unseen buildings. Again, I faced the rear of the building outward.

The two manufacturing buildings in the right center section were chosen for their windows sizes, **6-14**. Demonstrating the importance of relative window sizes, the N. B. Sougloff building is inches away from the O-scale buildings below it. The narrow structure to its left is another five-story Heljan brewery building, which sits on a 6" riser.

On the right side of the cityscape, there are only a few buildings. National Cold Storage, the building right of N. B. Sougloff Corp., was also chosen for its window size because it is almost on top of the O scale building below it, **6-15**. A variety of colors help delineate the buildings in this section.

Completing the atmosphere

The cityscape plays a prominent part in creating the big-city feel of the Sandy Harbor, but other elements were needed to complete the atmosphere that I was after. I needed to hang a backdrop, fill in some odd spaces, and add some scenery and gritty, city details.

Adding a backdrop

When you look at the cityscape, you should see sky. You could, of course, paint a backdrop or use photographic prints. But if you're looking for a simple and cost-effective way to create a smooth, continuous backdrop, using a roll of photo paper is an idea worth considering. The paper roll costs about 50 dollars and comes in many colors including various shades of blue. You can find it at any well-stocked photo store.

To add a sky around the Sandy Harbor, I used different intensities of blue light to shade the white photo backdrop paper. I hung the paper along the two walls that surrounded the layout, **6-16**. I first attached a 1" x 6" board horizontally to a rafter, letting it hang down about 3". This would serve as an attachment point for the paper. Then I had a friend unroll the paper, which was 36 feet long and 53" wide, as I stapled it along the top of the 1 x 6. About 3 feet from the corner, I allowed the paper to take a natural bend to the wall. Then I continued stapling the paper to the wall until I got to the end of the roll.

Big-city detail

Some of the neatest little details come about through a combination of opportunity and circumstance. I had several spaces to fill on the Sandy Harbor, and my favorite little gem has to be the building that is no longer there, **6-17**. This detail came about because I needed to fill an odd, empty area between two buildings. In one of my scrap boxes, I found some broken plaster wall pieces. I glued them together to form adjoining walls, so it looked like a building

had been torn down, and then I added some boards, pipes, and other debris to the lot.

A bland, triangular green space between two streets needed a little accent. I made a brick planter from kitbashed plastic HO brick pavement sections and added Woodland Scenics green fine weeds as plants. That was a good start, but it still needed something more. A Revolutionary War statue became a natural outgrowth and was prototypically suited to the location, **6-18**.

The statue is made from a plastic toy figure glued onto a wooden cube trimmed with dollhouse molding, **6-19**. First, I trimmed the figure's base to fit the cube and sprayed the blue figure with white primer. Then, after it dried, I sprayed the figure with Krylon Hammered Finish Brown Metallic paint (no. 2917). To add some relief to the block, I glued the molding around the top edge. Then I sprayed it with gray primer and very lightly misted with white primer to give it a granite texture. I then glued the figure to the block with cyanoacrylate adhesive.

A dead space between Garfield News and the tracks presented yet another challenge to make it shine. To give the small space some contrast, I put down a much-forgotten pile of rubble and surrounded it with a variety of vegetation, **6-20**. The ground cover mixture consisted of Brennan's Natural Earth and Rock Creek Sand; Woodland Scenics coarse turf, grass, and poly fiber; and Silflor Summer Pasture with Weeds.

In addition to offering some visual interest, these tiny accents provide a sense of history that gives added flavor to the present scene. In real life, everything has its counterpart—growth and decay, light and shadow, up and down, and even past and present. You can't have one without the other, and if you apply this obvious but often overlooked concept to your layout's reality, you've doubled your modeling options.

Adding more dimension

Although the little hobo shack on the leading edge of the Sandy Harbor could have been easily overshadowed by its industrial backdrop, it commands our attention, **6-21**. That's because it resides in a hollow that isolates it, and by doing so, emphasizes what lies beyond. Adding dimension to a layout provides emphasis and interest.

In flat areas alongside the track, the scenery base does not always have to remain on the same level as the track base. Railroads often use cuts and fills to keep their right-of-way as level as possible, **6-22**. Therefore, the trackside topography naturally rises and falls. To lower the track, simply raise the area alongside it. The simple addition of a single ceiling tile changes the elevation of the right-of-way, **6-23**.

Once again, I relied on nothing but regular old masking tape to form the slope. I know what you're thinking. Surely, I should put a layer of plaster, Celluclay, or something else over it. Well, it's not necessary. You can apply the paint and the scenery directly over the tape. And for small transitions like this, no underlying support is needed. The tape is surprisingly strong, and it does not get brittle nor lift up from the surface over time.

To start, I beveled the top edge of the ceiling tile bordering the right-of-way with a sanding sponge. This makes a smooth transition to the slope. For a more eroded look along the facing edge that runs perpendicular to the tracks, I broke some jagged pieces off the ceiling tile. Then I vacuumed the area to pick up the small particles.

In most applications, I put down 3"-wide masking tape in three overlapping layers of different directions. This adds strength and allows you to stretch out the slope if necessary. Certainly, I could have carved and sanded the ceiling tile to arrive at something similar. But, in this instance, the tape was quick, clean, and effective. Once you start using tape, you'll see how easy it is to manipulate.

When you're happy with the shape of the taped slope, it's time to give it a good coat of paint. I used my standard earth-colored paint and let it set up overnight before adding any scenery. Painting

6-12

These kitbashed industrial buildings show a variety of heights that add visual interest to the cityscape.

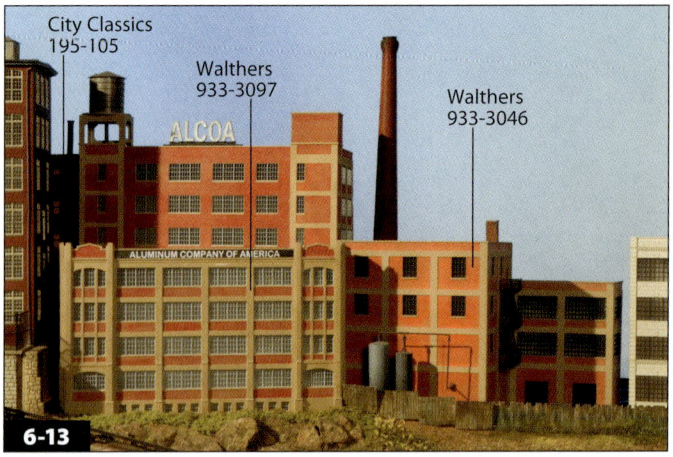

6-13

The Aluminum Company of America complex consists of several buildings that I made from Walthers American Hardware Supply (933-3097) and George Roberts Printing Company (933-3046) kits.

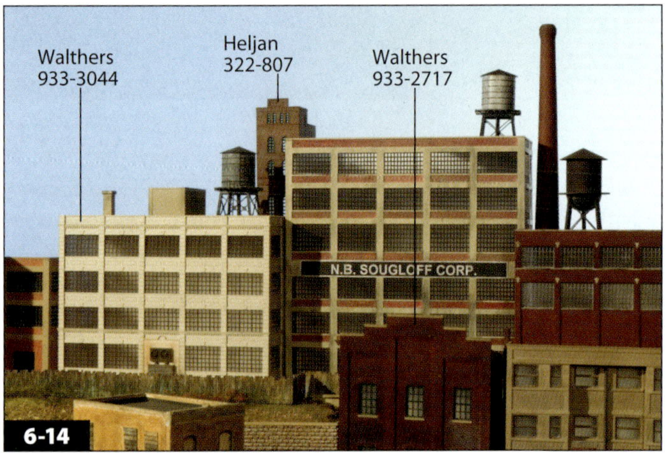

6-14

The building on the left is Walthers Hardwood Furniture (933-3044) The N. B. Sougloff Corp. building is kitbashed from the George Roberts Printing (933-3046) and Variety Printing (933-3252) kits.

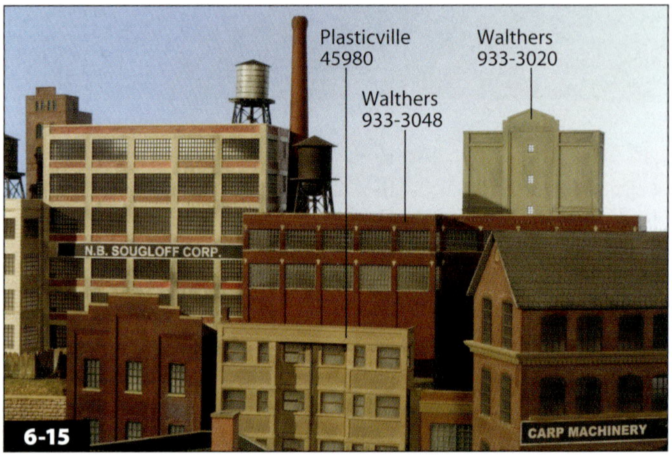

6-15

National Cold Storage, between N. B. Sougloff and Carp Machinery, is made from Walthers Champion Packing Plant (933-3048). I selected it because its windows matched well with the building in front of it.

seals the tape, increases its durability, and reinforces its bond to the surrounding area. After painting, the tape may start to wrinkle. This is normal, and the wrinkles will disappear when the paint dries completely.

The next day, I added a second coat of paint and immediately added scenery: a combination of Brennan's Natural Earth (fine and underbrush) and Woodland Scenics static grass flock (burnt grass). I like to do the scenery before ballasting for two reasons: this way, the ballast naturally sits on top of the ground cover, and dirty washes applied to the ballast leach out into the scenery to create a natural blend. However, even for a weed-encroached right-of-way, it's easy enough to add additional ground cover on top of the ballast. The application of scenery doesn't have to be a one-time process.

Scenery tips

You don't have to be an artist to make convincing scenery. We all learn by doing. The secret is to avoid uniformity. There is hardly anything in the real world that is all one color or one texture. While one color and texture may seem to predominate in a grassy field, upon closer inspection, you may find scrubby burnt-green vegetation, tall green and yellow wild grasses, purple thistle, delicate blue wild flowers, white clover, brown brambles, and leafy green bushes as well as thatch, dirt, and rocks.

Complete your scenery one texture level at a time. Start by adding the finer textures and work your way up to the coarse ones. Randomly sprinkle different colors in various concentrations. Start with light amounts since you can always add more. And when you're finished, you should still be able to see some dirt.

Once you're satisfied with your handiwork, use a spray bottle to gently mist everything with "wet water," water with about four drops of dish detergent in it. Depending on the area, sometimes it's easier to use a squeeze bottle with a pointed tip. This soaking agent reduces the surface tension of water, which allows glue to be easily absorbed and evenly distributed throughout the scenery.

Next, gently apply the bonding solution with another applicator bottle. The tips on spray bottles often clog when used with glue mixtures, so I avoid them. I use a mixture of one part white glue to two or three parts water and a few drops of dish detergent. Completely saturate the area until everything turns milky white. Although it may look messy, when it dries, the mixture becomes invisible.

Some people use matte medium rather than white glue. The reasoning is

Photo paper forms a smooth, continuous backdrop. I let the background buildings extend slightly beyond the rear edge of the layout to give them more room. The openings in the foam allow access to the track.

Tucked away in a corner, the remnants of an old building mark the passage of time. Some broken plaster castings, a few pieces of lumber, and other items from the scrap box combine to create the scene.

that matte medium dries without leaving any shine. That's true enough, but I see no discernible difference. While white glue may leave a slight sheen when used full strength, when it's diluted, that's not an issue. Another consideration is that white glue can be resoftened with water while matte medium is permanent.

Digging deeper

A railroad culvert provides another way to add dimension to a flat scene. I decided to place a culvert on the other side of the track behind Garfield News. I began by making a straight cut in the foam with a serrated knife and then removed enough foam to insert the culvert. With the culvert in place, it was easy to determine the shape of the accompanying drainage ditch. Creating a drainage ditch is easy. First, cut out a small space for the casting and use the casting as a guide to carve out the ditch, **6-24**.

With that done, I added a base coat of paint and set to work applying the initial ground cover. I sprinkled on some Brennan's fine-grade Natural Earth and then filled in with the coarse grade, **6-25**. Generally, if I'm covering a hillside, such as here, I'll use more of the coarse grade, but if it's a level surface, I'll use more of the fine grade. The coarse grade helps hold additional textures in place while bonding with the glue mixture. The main thing is to vary the texture and amount of the ground cover. And don't be afraid to let a little paint show through here and there as it becomes yet another texture. Applying ground cover is simple and goes quickly, and you'll quickly see the area start to come alive.

Grasses, weeds, and shrubbery come next. For this particular area, I freely combined natural and commercial products to produce a variety of colors and textures, **6-26**.

Woodland Scenics is a very popular brand of commercial ground foam, and one that I frequently use. However, other brands work equally well. Here, I included various green fine and coarse turfs along with Woodland Scenics purple Flowering Foliage.

I also used natural moss that I found right in my own backyard, **6-27**. The moss is very easy to harvest—it comes up in sheet-like clumps and has very little dirt attached. Because the moss has a very dense root system, it stays together quite well. I used regular white glue to hold it in place on the layout. I did nothing to process it, and it's been on the layout for more than two years and has not become brittle or lost its color.

To cover the creek bed, I used a mixture of my fine-grade Superior Sand and Rock Creek Sand. For some larger rocks, I threw in a few pebbles from a nearby creek. A cosmetic clear nail hardener is a good choice for modeling small bodies of water such as puddles or a tiny stream. I built up the water with several brush-on applications, as it's important to let the hardener dry between coats. Although you might be tempted to pour on the hardener, that is not a good idea since it will not set properly, and the results will be unsatisfactory.

An Arttista figure sitting by the Revolutionary War statue provides a sense of scale.

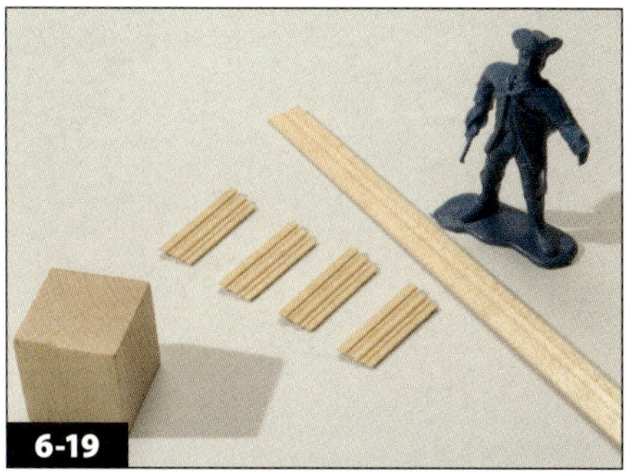

The elements for making a statue came from Hobby Lobby. The molding is dollhouse trim, and the 1" block is from the crafts department. After starting the statue, I replaced this plastic figure with one I thought looked better.

6-20

This triangular space was too small for anything more than an empty lot, but it didn't have to be completely empty. The pile of bricks and stones comes from Custom Dioramics (1:35 scale rubble CD0401).

6-21

This hobo shack was inspired by a childhood adventure. One summer day, my best friend, Bobby, and I stumbled across two 'bos. They had stories to tell and kept us spellbound for hours. If mom only knew…

6-22

This cut is only a ½" rise, but it is amazing how much even a small change in elevation adds to the realism.

6-23

A ceiling tile and masking tape form the basis of a tiny cut along the right-of-way. Using masking tape is a quick and easy way to form a gentle slope.

6-24

I purposely left the drainage ditch rough as the uneven terrain looks like natural erosion.

6-25

There's a striking difference once the paint and initial ground cover are added to the ditch.

6-26

The seemingly random distribution of colors and textures produces a totally natural look. The wispy weeds are painted fun fur.

6-27

I carefully removed tiny pieces of natural moss, coated them with regular white glue, and pressed the pieces onto the foam.

6-28

To obtain a pleasing overall shape, rearrange the rocks until you find a combination that looks natural.

6-29

Celluclay fills in the gaps and ties the individual rocks together.

6-30

Greenery adds contrast and brings life to the scene. Defined by the absence of ground cover, a footpath runs along the stone wall.

6-31

Realistic scenery is done through transparent blending and subtle variations. There are no real hard lines between the ballast, greenery, and the layout's edge.

Climbing ol' rocky top

I created a rocky outcrop to justify having tunnels and a hillside. As I did for the harbor scene, I made use of real rocks and arranged them above the tunnels, **6-28**. Only this time, I used much bigger pieces. I mixed a batch of Celluclay with brown latex paint to use as mortar and for creating the hillside around the rocks, **6-29**.

I brushed the rocks with an India ink and alcohol mixture (one tablespoon of ink to one pint of rubbing alcohol). This darkens their natural color and brings out the detail. To finish the hillside, I added a ground cover of Brennan's fine Natural Earth, Woodland Scenics fine and coarse turf (burnt grass), and Silflor Flowering Meadows, **6-30**. I used white glue as a bonding agent.

Using organic materials

Scenery experts have long used natural materials to enhance realism. The trick is

Extending the scenery below the front edge of the layout gives rise to dramatic low angle shots like this. There are only about 5" of space between the track and the front of the rocks.

finding the right stuff. I've used ground-up pine needles, leaves, acorns, and other natural materials. Sandy soils also work well for ground cover. Most soils require a bit of sifting, which is best done outside. And if anything is wet or damp, just let the sun dry it out. Don't use your oven to remove moisture or treat your recycled goodies. No one will appreciate the natural odor that permeates the kitchen. Suffice to say, I don't even think about using the oven or any of my wife's appliances for something other than a food product.

Scenic effects

Completing the foreground scenery along the layout's edge was one of the last things that I did. And what a difference—I knew it would finally make the layout look finished, but even I was amazed at just how much more it added to the overall effect. Realistic looking scenery is all about transparent blending and subtle variation. On its journey around the layout, I varied the ground cover with changes in color, texture, and type, **6-31**.

From the layout's start, I resisted the temptation to run the track right up to the edge of the layout. This would also be the one area where I could add a considerable amount of greenery as a counterpart to the city's brick, steel, concrete, and stone. I also reasoned that it would give me greater photographic flexibility if I had more foreground scenery between the edge of the table and the track. And by having the scenery base slope down and away from the track, I could even place the camera slightly lower than track level, **6-32**.

Adding some real rocks along the front of the layout was a simple process. The first step was cutting out a shelf for the rocks with a serrated knife. I then placed the rocks in a pleasing pattern, **6-33**. Next, I used some Celluclay mixed with brown latex paint to join the rocks and blend them into the surrounding foam, **6-34**. I top coated the Celluclay with more brown latex paint and sprinkled Rock Creek Sand over it to create a seamless transition from the rocks to the roadbed, **6-35**. It is often easier to complete the ground cover before you ballast the track.

An area alongside another culvert seemed like a good place for some undergrowth and flowering bushes, **6-36**. First, I applied Brennan's Natural Earth undergrowth over a coat of brown paint. I then sprayed it with Krylon clear matte spray and immediately applied stretched-out Woodland Scenics green poly fiber. The red flowers are bits of colored foam that I picked up someplace, but you could use Woodland Scenics fall red coarse turf.

Farther along the railside, I created a different look by using a dark green, thin, flexible kitchen scrubbing pad that I pulled apart. I randomly sprinkled Woodland Scenics fine and coarse light green turf to blend it in and added a white flowering plant from a Silfor Flowering Meadows sampler pack, **6-37**.

I wanted the hillside around and behind the hobo shack to be overgrown. The thicket is a combination of Woodland Scenics green poly fiber, harvest gold static grass flock, and light green coarse turf, **6-38**.

6-33

I cut out just enough foam to hold the full-size rocks.

6-34

Work the Celluclay between and around the rocks to cement them in position and blend everything together.

6-35

The final ground cover creates a seamless transition from roadbed to rock face. I worked the scenery up to the track before ballasting.

6-36

To add flowers to the bushes, I attached pieces of red foam with matte spray.

6-37

You never know what will make good scenery material. The dark green foliage is from a thin kitchen scrubbing pad that I pulled apart.

6-38

Green poly fiber, gold static grass, and light green turf combined to produce an overgrown area near the hobo shack.

A final flourish

The beveled strip of foreground scenery had another effect that I hadn't considered. It combined with the smooth flowing curves of the tabletop to elegantly frame the layout. Black velvet skirting hides the benchwork and keeps your eyes focused on the layout. My wife, Sandy, made 45"-wide overlapping, removable panels, which we secured with Velcro hook and loop fabric. Sandy sewed the loops to the panels while I stapled the hooks to the fascia.

Now that we've gone over how a big city should look, in the next chapter, I'll describe one of my favorite activities, kitbuilding, which is one of the fundamental skills for building a city, big or small.

7-1

Sticks and stones

These are just a few of the many structure kits I've acquired from various manufacturers over the years. They encompass a wide range of materials.

Building models can be one of the most enjoyable and satisfying aspects of the hobby. I think some people shy away from building kits because they've never done it or they may have had a bad kit-building experience. One problem with kits is that some instructions assume that you know more than you do. These instructions may be perplexing for beginning builders, which often leads to frustration. Hopefully, I can clear up any confusion by giving you some good basic information regarding kits, glue, and painting. Then I'll illustrate various construction techniques by taking you step-by-step through several projects. None of this is beyond your capabilities—all it requires is a little patience.

Kit choices

Many of you are probably familiar with Plasticville snap-together kits by Bachmann. These simple plastic kits have been a staple on toy train layouts since their introduction in the early '50s. Back then, Marx and Littletown also produced plastic buildings, and Skyline offered some tin lithographed and cardboard buildings. Today, however, we have many more choices, **7-1**. Dozens of large and small manufacturers produce kits in plastic, resin, wood, plaster, cardboard, and paper. A quick count on the Valley Model Trains Web site (www.valleymodeltrains.com) shows more than 70 suppliers.

If you're new to kit-building, I suggest starting with a basic plastic kit from Bachmann, Ameri-Towne, or Korber. Many of these kits contain little more than four walls and a roof. As you gain experience, you can move on to more advanced plastic, resin, wood, and plaster kits. Don't worry about whether you can build a particular kit. If you like it, go ahead and buy it. The day will come when you're ready. I still have several kits bought long before I knew what I was doing.

Plastic-injection molded kits. These kits range from simple snap-together Plasticville kits with cast-in details to more elaborate Atlas O kits having lots of add-on pieces. Kits by Ameri-Towne and Korber are somewhere in between, **7-2**.

Plaster kits. Plaster kits are usually made from a dense plaster such as Hydrocal, which is a very pure form of plaster of paris. Normally, what is sold in building supply stores as plaster of paris has other additives. A typical plaster kit consists of plaster walls with separately applied detail parts for doors and windows, **7-3**.

The walls are hand-poured into individual molds, and they may contain slight imperfections, such as tiny holes or small round nubs. These are caused by air bubbles in the plaster or in the molds. You can easily pick off the little nubs by hand or with a round toothpick. Any holes can be filled with spackle or just cut away and blended in with a hobby knife.

Although the individual castings are fragile, once a kit is built, it's quite sturdy. I made the mistake once of laying

7-2

This polystyrene Ameri-Towne (Acme Machine no. 442) kit consists of four walls with cast-in windows and doors, a roof, and some detail parts.

7-3

Hand-poured plaster kits don't have the precision machined edges like plastic injected molded kits. But it is this organic quality and the way plaster absorbs color that adds to their realism. This wall is from the Universal Supply Factory kit by Brennan's Model Railroading.

7-4

Resin kits are hand-poured like plaster but more closely related to plastic when it comes to painting. Like many resin kits, this kit by Design Preservation Models has cast-in windows and doors.

7-5 The assembly of a laser-cut wood kit is not necessarily difficult but certainly requires more work on your part. This is an Elevated Crossing Shanty by Building & Structure Co.

7-6 Randsburg Barbershop is a laser-cut paper craftsman kit by Paper Creek Model Works (www.Papercreek.com) These kits produce extremely realistic models without any painting or weathering. Once they are assembled, you're done.

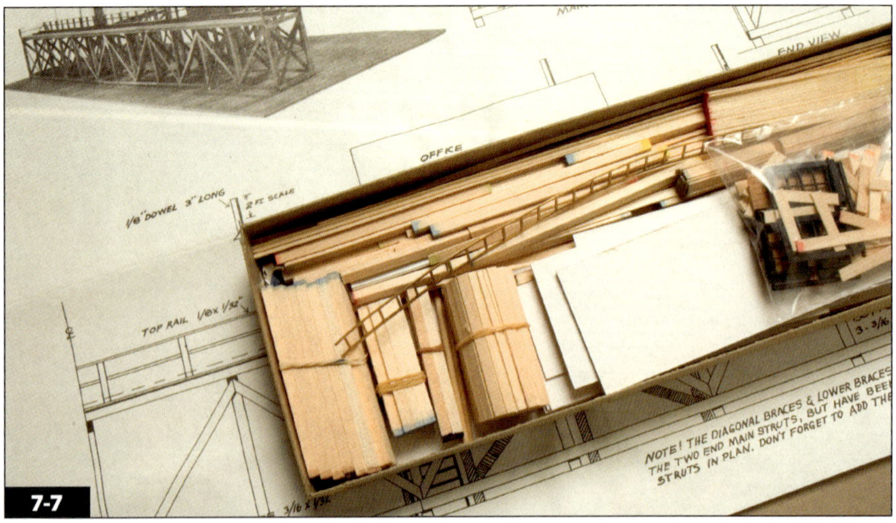

7-7 This traditional craftsman kit by Suncoast Models contains stripwood, cardstock, brass, and plastic detail parts. The wood pieces are color coded for easy identification. After you've built a kit like this, you can tackle anything.

a kit wall on top of something and then inadvertently leaned on it. You can guess what happened. However, if you do happen to break a casting, don't panic. It is easily glued back together. And, if you wish, you can also patch the crack with spackle—it will just add character to your building. Cracks, patches, chips, and broken pieces are normal in real brick and concrete structures.

I remember the first time I ever opened a plaster kit: my main concern was how to color the stark white plaster castings. Well, not to worry. It's actually easier to achieve a realistic masonry look with plaster than it is with precolored plastic. There are many different ways to color plaster. Some kits suggest prepainting with white spray paint and then painting as you would normally. Others suggest first sealing with clear lacquer and then applying solvent-based stains. Still others recommend using water-based stains on raw plaster. I prefer the latter approach. By not sealing the plaster, you take advantage of the fact that plaster may not absorb color evenly. This imparts a natural variation in tone that looks especially good on masonry and stonework. And the beauty is that you don't have to be an artist to achieve realistic results.

For an orange brick color, I recommend using Higgins russet drawing ink at full strength. For a yellow-brown brick, try Minwax English Oak stain. You can also use artists' acrylic tube colors. Don't be afraid to experiment with any water-based color but first test it on the back of the casting and let it dry before evaluating the results.

Resin kits. Resin kits are made from polyester or polyurethane, which are both impervious to plastic cements and other solvents. The castings are hand-poured into individual molds similar to how plaster kits are made, **7-4**. And like plaster castings, they may have slight imperfections from trapped air bubbles. These tiny spots can be filled with Squadron Green Putty or carved and blended with a knife. Again, any imperfections only add character to a building. Typically, resin kits have cast-in windows and doors.

Sometimes you may find a warped casting. A wall can usually be straightened by laying it on its back on a solid

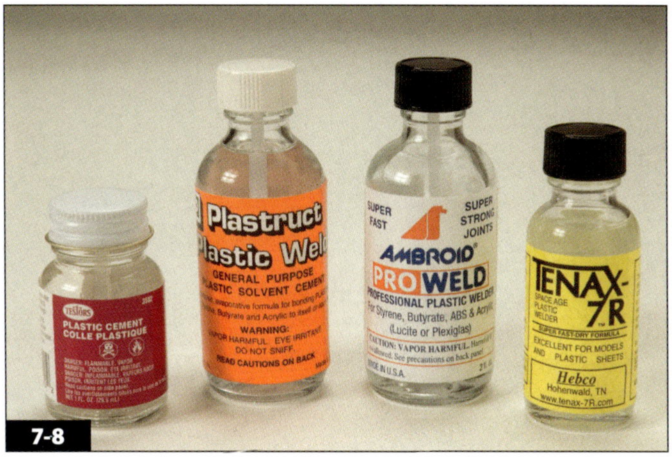

7-8

One or more of these liquid cements can usually be found on any plastic kit builder's workbench. These solvents are much easier to use, and they produce consistently better results than plastic tube-type cements.

7-9

Good old Elmer's wood glue and regular white Glue-All should be other staples in your glue arsenal. They are great for art board, ceiling tiles, cork, foam, Homasote, plaster, and wood.

flat surface, placing a weight on it, and leaving it sit for a day. I have also straightened walls by clamping and gluing a ¼" square piece of hardwood across the back with epoxy. As a last resort, you might try carefully heating it with a hair dryer until it relaxes, but never use a heat gun unless you want to melt the wall.

Wood kits. Wood kits fall into two categories: what I call "stick kits" and laser-cut kits. Stick kits are made of stripwood and may include some basswood siding. The pieces may or may not be precut. Laser-cut kits are typically built up in layers and may have tabs and slots for joining various parts. Trim pieces and windows are often peel-and-stick, and most everything is precut, including the walls, **7-5**. Normally, these finely detailed kits are painted prior to assembly. Since the wood is very thin, you should add braces to the interior side of the walls prior to painting, and the walls should also be painted or stained on both sides to prevent warping. Although there's more assembly required compared to plastic, plaster, or resin kits, your efforts will produce an eye-catching model that begs close examination.

Paper kits. These kits consist of illustrations printed on heavy paper, **7-6**. The graphics range from simple artwork to photorealistic renderings. Assembly usually requires minimal tools—mainly a straightedge, hobby knife, white glue, and tweezers. They're typically built up in layers to add dimension. Some kits feature laser-cut paper and may include pieces with adhesive backings to aid in assembly. Other than coloring the raw, white

Keys to kit-building

Patience is the key to producing an outstanding model—so take your time and enjoy the building process. The following points should be standard operating procedure for assembling any kit.

- **Read instructions.** Read the instructions before doing anything else. Identify all the pieces as you go. This will give you a basic understanding of how everything fits together as well as providing the assembly sequence. While what goes where may be obvious, oftentimes the order isn't. You may have to read the instructions over several times before you completely understand them.

- **Separate pieces.** Always cut, rather than break, plastic parts off their sprues. If you snap them off, you run the risk of damaging the pieces. Also, it's best to leave small parts attached to the sprue until you're ready to use them. That way they're easy to identify, easy to paint, and less likely to get lost.

- **Check parts.** Look over the parts carefully. Remove any flash and parting seams. Parting seams appear as a very thin ridge of plastic. These are formed where the upper and lower halves of the mold come together. Check the fit to make sure all parts mate properly. Even the simplest snap-together Plasticville kit may need a little sanding and filing to ensure tightly jointed corners or seams.

- **Clean kits.** Always wash plastic and resin kits prior to painting. This removes any residual mold-release compound and any oils that result from handling. Paint does not adhere well to mold-release agents. To clean plastic kits, gently scrub the pieces with a toothbrush using warm water and liquid dish detergent. To clean resin kits, gently scrub them with a toothbrush using mineral spirits or Goo Gone and then repeat the step with liquid dish soap and warm water. Soap and water alone will not remove most resin mold-release agents.

- **Select glue.** There are many adhesives available. Use the right glue for the job. Using the wrong glue can lead to problems down the road.

- **Replace blade.** Always start with a fresh blade in your hobby knife and change it often. Sharp blades make cleaner cuts, which results in easier assembly and less damage to pieces, especially smaller ones.

- **Add glazing.** Install window glazing as the last step in the assembly process. This simplifies painting and lessens handling of the building during construction.

- **Square walls.** For the best fit, and a good-looking building, use a carpenter's square to ensure that walls are perpendicular to each other when gluing them together.

- **Paint interior.** Many plastic and resin kits are translucent. If you intend to light the interior, paint the interior walls flat black before painting the exterior.

7-10

When you have to bond dissimilar materials, one of these three all-purpose glues fits the bill.

7-11

Regular primers, flats, and satins are inexpensive and produce excellent results on plastic models. I especially like the camouflage colors for their ultra flat finish.

paper edges, no painting is necessary since they're essentially finished. A big advantage of these kits is their low cost.

Craftsman kits. Sometimes a kit may be referred to as a craftsman kit. What exactly is a craftsman kit? Well, if you open a box full of pieces, and you absolutely have to read the instructions to make any sense at all out of it, then you just might have a craftsman kit, **7-7**. These kits normally contain detailed scale-sized drawings and templates to aid in assembly.

Bonding guide

Using manufacturer information, here is a short guide to what materials some liquid plastic cements can be used with.

- **Testors Plastic Cement:** glues polystyrene (plastic models), ABS (acrylonitrile butadiene styrene), acetate, plexiglass, and other plastics
- **Plastruct Plastic Weld:** bonds ABS, styrene, butyrate, or acrylic to each other or in combination
- **Plastruct Bondene:** bonds styrene to styrene, ABS to ABS, and other similar plastic applications
- **Hebco Tenax-7R:** bonds models and plastic sheets; is super fast—bonds in about 10 seconds

In these applications, styrene can be considered identical to polystyrene. The two words are often used interchangeably. Styrene is actually a liquid. Polystyrene is made from polymerized styrene.

Craftsman kits have been a staple of the hobby for more than 60 years. Prior to World War II, before the advent of plastic-injection molding, scratch-building was standard for scale model railroaders. Buildings were commonly fashioned from basswood and artist's illustration board. This took quite a bit of craftsmanship. The modeler had to draw up his plans, usually based upon an existing structure, gather the materials, and then figure out how to put it together. The kits of that day utilized the same approach. The difference being that the design and assembly process were already figured out, and many pieces were precut. The modeler was still the builder, just not the architect.

Today, the concept remains the same, but there are many more raw materials to work with. Craftsman kits may consist of one material such as wood, art board, or styrene, but more often, they contain combinations of stripwood, styrene, art board, and plaster along with plastic, resin, or metal detail parts. These kits are not necessarily difficult to build—they simply require patience. They're also more expensive due to the instructions, design, and fabrication that go into their production.

Selecting glues

Glue is the single most important component needed when assembling models, and using the right adhesive for a kit's materials is critical. If you check out the glue section in a hardware store, you'll find a dizzying selection—most of which are overkill for our modeling needs.

The following glue types are commonly used in model-making: liquid plastic cement, white glue and yellow wood glue, and all-purpose adhesives including instant glue, 5-minute epoxy, and contact cement such as Walther's Goo.

Liquid plastic cement

There are several brands of liquid plastic cement, **7-8**. These adhesives melt the surface of plastic, so the softened pieces fuse together to make a permanent bond. Most are general-purpose solvents that are suitable for bonding various types of plastic to each other, but some, such as Bondene, only bond like plastics. I've used them all, but I favor Plastruct Plastic Weld. My advice is to try each one to see which works best for you.

These bonding agents are volatile, and they will lose their potency when left uncapped. When I've encountered a problem, it's usually due to one of two things: either the solvent is too old, or it's not suitable for the particular plastic.

Unlike tube-type plastic cements, the liquids form an invisible bond, and you can simply apply them with a brush to the back of the joined pieces. Capillary action and very gentle pressure pull the solvent into the joint. Be aware that paint acts as a barrier and must be removed from the mating surfaces before gluing.

Using the correct amount of liquid plastic cement can be tricky. You don't want to slop it on, but there has to be enough to melt the plastic. Don't worry if a little softened plastic oozes out of a joint. Simply let it dry completely and then scrape it off with a hobby knife.

You may need to do a little light sanding to remove a blemish, but once it's painted, you'll never see it.

White and yellow glues

For wood and plaster kits, I recommend Elmer's carpenter's wood glue or Titebond, **7-9**. Although similar to regular white glue, the yellow wood glues are tackier and set up faster. Both yellow and white glues are water-soluble, which makes it easy for cleaning up any errant glue. Since these glues will seal plaster or wood, I suggest staining or painting plaster and wood pieces prior to assembly. These glues are also good for bonding construction foam, foam core, cardstock, cork, Homasote, and ceiling tiles.

7-12

The Plasticville suburban station adorned many 1950s toy train layouts.

All-purpose adhesives

There are three main types of all-purpose adhesives commonly used in modeling: cyanoacrylate adhesive, epoxy, and contact cement, **7-10**.

Cyanoacrylate adhesive. Cyanoacrylate adhesive (CA) is the general term for instant-setting glues such as Super Glue, Hot Stuff, Zap, and Krazy Glue. It comes in both liquid and gel forms. Although CA will bond almost everything, including your fingers, it is especially useful when you need to join dissimilar materials. I typically use it when adding plastic detail parts to plaster or wood kits. I also use it to repair broken plaster castings. I have found the gel works better than the liquid when joining plaster to plaster. The trick when using liquid adhesive with plaster is to first coat each piece to seal it, join them together, and then reapply the glue to the seam. Capillary action pulls the liquid CA into the joint.

CA also seals plaster and wood just as wood glue does. So, again I suggest staining plaster or wood before bonding it. And, since it has no shear strength, and won't withstand any lateral force, I'll often use it when kitbashing plastic kits. That way I can separate wall pieces if necessary. It also works with resin kits. Acetone will remove CA from model pieces and fingers.

You should always use CA in a well-ventilated room. The fumes can irritate your eyes, nose, and throat. It can also craze (crack) clear plastic including plastic eyewear.

7-13

What a transformation! A few minor changes turn a simple plastic kit into an eye-catching model that is home on even the most detailed hi-rail layout.

Epoxy. A 5-minute epoxy consists of a hardener and a resin that need to be thoroughly mixed in equal proportions before using. It comes in two separate tubes or in a double-plunger dispenser. 5-minute epoxy is often the recommended adhesive for resin kits, although CA works just as well. Epoxy can also be used to bond plaster. However, make sure the plaster is thoroughly dry before gluing. Otherwise, the epoxy won't stick. I found that out the hard way. Sometimes, I'll use CA to join kit walls and then put a fillet of epoxy along the inside corner where it won't be seen. Epoxy also cleans up with acetone.

Contact cement. Contact cement is great for bonding dissimilar materials. This durable, rubber-based glue tends to be stringy, so I prefer to use it on hidden joints where it's not likely to be seen. It is removable with acetone.

Some thoughts about painting

Generally, you want to handle a structure as little as possible after painting, so try to do any cutting, sanding, or altering first. Then, depending on the kit, the walls may be painted either before or after they're assembled. There are no hard and fast rules. If the windows, trim, and other details are cast into the walls, I find it easier to paint the walls prior to assembly. In that case, I'll usually spray on the basic wall color first. After that dries, I'll repaint the windows.

7-14 **When the sandpaper needs to be replaced on the cutting board, I scrape off the sandpaper, apply a little Goo Gone to the board to get rid of the remaining glue, give the board a wash, and it's good to go.**

7-15 **Applying drywall joint compound to the plastic surface creates a realistic stucco texture as shown on the bottom wall.**

Spray painting is an effective way to paint almost anything. I have an airbrush but seldom use it. I have been using spray paint for more than 20 years and have obtained excellent results.

If you stick with a flat or satin finish or a primer, regular spray paint works just fine, **7-11**. These paints are compatible with both plastic and resin kits and adhere nicely. It is not necessary to use spray paints designed specifically for plastics. These paints were developed to provide a durable, weather-resistant finish for slick plastic outdoor furniture.

Spray-painting tips

Here are five simple tips on how to spray paint effectively:

- Before spraying, prevent clogging by shaking the can for three minutes after the mixing ball starts rattling.
- Hold the can 12" to 18" away from the surface.
- Do not cover with a continuous spray. Move back and forth in a straight line, releasing the spray head after each stroke. You want to apply a very fine mist, not a heavy coat.
- Your strokes should begin and end on either side of the object. Do not start and stop the spray on the piece.
- After spraying, always invert the can and spray until the mist is clear. This keeps the paint from drying in the tube and rendering the can useless.

You may hear that regular spray paint attacks the plastic in models, but I've never had a problem. Here's the deal—the solvents in the paint can indeed cause fine surface cracks commonly called crazing. However, this only happens if you apply a heavy coat. Even if crazing wasn't an issue, you don't want to cover with a heavy coat. It obscures fine details and is often the ruination of an otherwise good model.

The goal is to cover without splatters or runs. Err on the side of applying too little paint. You can always add more. I suggest that you practice on a piece of paper until you get a feel for the technique and the spray pattern. Believe it or not, spray cans do not spray the same.

The trick is to apply several light coats, gradually building up the coverage. Applying light coats allows most of the solvent to disperse before the paint hits the plastic. Also, check the manufacturer's recommended timeframe for applying additional coats. It may be something like "within one hour or after 48 hours." Heed that advice. That's because, after an hour, the paint has sufficiently set up, so extra coats will seal in the underlying solvent and keep the paint from drying properly. It takes 48 hours for the solvent to completely dissipate.

Assembling kits

The intent of the following projects is not so much for you to copy what I did, although that is certainly a viable option. It is more to provide ideas and inspiration by showing you my approach to assembling three different types of kits. When completed and on the layout, I don't think anyone will notice any distinction between the simple snap-together plastic station, the resin grocery wholesaler, and the craftsman restaurant. Hopefully, you'll see that you don't have to be a master craftsman to obtain masterful results. All it takes is some patience and a little willingness to think outside the box.

Snap-together suburban station

This Plasticville kit was first produced by Bachmann (www.bachmanntrains.com) in 1950 and can still be found on many layouts today, **7-12**. Originally, I set out to show how you could enhance a plastic kit's appearance with the simple addition of some paint and a little weathering. Well, one thing led to another, and I ended up with a realistic depot that belies its toy train heritage, **7-13**. This is a perfect illustration of how any project can evolve from its initial concept. Once I got started, new ideas came about. I could have stopped at any step along the way and still had a nice model.

Although it's a simple snap-together kit, we'll use the same basic assembly techniques that apply to even the most complex model. The first step is to check the fit of the four walls. The pieces should abut with no obvious gaps. To get a close fit, you may have to file or sand the inside edges of the side walls. I use a piece of 100-grit, wet or dry sandpaper spray-glued to the smooth side of a glass cutting board, **7-14**. Lightly draw the edge across the paper a time or two and then check the fit, repeating as necessary. You may also have to file the alignment tabs for a good fit.

Speaking of cutting boards, which might seem a little unusual, I bought a Farberware three-piece glass cutting board set just for modeling work. Glass cutting boards are ideal because they're solid, perfectly flat, and impervious to chemicals.

The problem with precolored plastic kits is that they have a plastic sheen. Getting rid of the shine is the first step in creating a realistic-looking structure. My plan was to spray the walls with Krylon Tan Camouflage spray and the doors and windows with Forest Green Camouflage. However, the simulated stucco wall texture was a little coarse for my taste, so I used drywall joint compound to smooth it out by simply smearing the compound across the wall with my finger, **7-15**. I used a toothpick to remove excess compound from the inset window and door areas and from underneath the sills. The great thing about joint compound is that it's water-soluble and, therefore, easy to remove. Don't use spackle; it's not the same thing.

Next, I spray-painted the walls. After they dried, I brush-painted over the cast-in windows. To do this, I simply decanted some green camo spray into a small container. The trick here is to have some paint thinner handy to help keep your brush pliable. While the windows were drying, I tackled the station's loading dock.

I wanted to add some wood grain to the platform by scraping a fine-tooth hobby saw across the surface and then painting it. But as I looked at it, the thought occurred to me that it would be simple enough to cover up the loading dock with scale lumber. And by letting the boards slightly hang over the deck, I could give it some extra dimension. Just that one decision led to the character-laden dock that adds so much to this model. I used ¹⁄₁₆" x ¼" stripwood (scale 3" x 12") for the deck boards and .020" x .156" stripwood (scale 1" x 8") for the horizontal boards underneath the platform (.156" actually scales out to 7½" and that's close enough).

I stained the wood with Minwax American Walnut water-based stain before doing anything else. To get varied

7-16

The original plastic dock provides the perfect substructure for the wood facade. What could be easier?

7-17

The Grandt Line double-hung windows are a major improvement over the cast-in windows.

7-18

I inserted the window from the back because the frame is unnecessary on a masonry building. It's also upside down. This protypically places the upper sash in front of the lower sash when viewed from the front.

7-19 To cut out the cast-in window, first score a groove around the window with the back of a hobby knife. The resulting groove helps guide the blade during the final cutting.

7-20 The two single wood doors turn into a double freight door (left). The double six-pane door casting becomes into two single-pane office doors.

7-21 A carpenter's square ensures perpendicular walls. Here, I've joined the front with a side. Next, I'll join the back with the other side wall. Then I'll join the two halves. If each half is square, the building will be square. The ¼" square strip of wood across the top of the wall acts as a stiffener.

tones, I used a cloth to randomly apply the stain to the stripwood before cutting. I made quick work of cutting the boards with a Northwest Shortline Chopper, a handy tool for accurately cutting stripwood or styrene. I cut the deck boards long enough to overhang the horizontal boards underneath. I allowed about the thickness of a board for the overhang.

Before gluing on the wood, I sawed off one ramp, so trucks had a place for backing up to the dock. Then, starting at one end of the deck, I super-glued each board into position and then attached the horizontal boards, **7-16**.

Once the dock was completed, I returned to the station's walls. It was at this point that I decided to replace the cast-in windows with Grandt Line scale windows (no. 3766). The overly large muntins (strips between glass panes) bothered me, and I found a slightly taller window that perfectly fit the width, **7-17**.

The 28" x 64" double-hung windows are made for wood-sided structures and are normally inserted from the front. But because this is a masonry structure, the window frame is superfluous, so I inserted the windows from the back, **7-18**.

To create the opening for the Grandt Line windows, I cut out the cast-in windows with a hobby knife. This is not difficult, but it does require a little patience. The first step is to score the plastic with the back of the knife blade, **7-19**. Starting at one corner, I worked my way around the edge of the window. I did this several times and then reversed direction. This ensures a clean corner-cut, and the resultant groove helps guide the knife blade. Next, I made repeated passes with the knife blade until it cut through the back of the casting. After removing the window, I enlarged the opening by cutting upward with a saw blade in my hobby knife. A few licks with a file cleans up the rough edges.

When I was satisfied that each window fit correctly, I set them aside for painting and turned my attention to the doors. I made three minor modifications that completely changed their look. I started by reversing the door configuration. I took the double six-pane door casting and split it into two separate doors. I then cut the muntins from those doors so they became single-pane office doors. Finally, I joined the two single "solid-wood" doors into a double freight door. I added .040" x .125" Evergreen strip styrene (no. 146) to fill in the flanges on the door sides, **7-20**. These strips provide a flush gluing surface and create a small reveal around the doors. This required the removal of the cast-in nubs from the back of the doorway openings.

Next, I joined two station walls together. I have found that the easiest way to get a square building is to bond a front or a back wall together with a side and then join the two halves. I'll often use a carpenter's square to ensure perpendicular walls, **7-21**. To bond two walls, apply a little glue at the top inside corner. Don't try to do the entire seam in one application. Use slight hand pressure to push the sides together and add more glue as you work your way down the wall.

Before joining the two halves, I installed the now-painted windows. For the glass, I used .030" clear acrylic sheet left over from a previous project. Both Plastruct and Evergreen offer .010" and .015" clear sheets for this purpose.

After getting this far, I thought that the roof overhang seemed overly large. My first thought was to cut it down, but then I remembered there was similar roof on a Korber trackside shanty in my stash of yet-to-be-built kits. To my amazement, it fit perfectly. To color the roof, I first sprayed it with white primer and let it dry. Then, I washed it with an India ink and alcohol weathering solution. I let this dry and repeated the process until I was satisfied with the effect.

I added a concrete chimney made from Evergreen styrene square tubing and a piece of strip styrene as the lip. To complete the project, I fashioned downspouts from 18 gauge floral stem wire and brackets made from eye pins, **7-22**.

So you see, with a little effort and some thinking from outside the box, you can take even a simple plastic kit to another level. Modifying a kit like this station is a great way to develop your modeling skills without breaking the bank.

7-22

The downspouts add detail and cover the corner joints in the walls.

Wholesale grocers resin kit

This polyurethane resin kit by DSL Shops (www.dslshops.com) is based on a scratch-built model created by pioneering model railroader Frank Ellison for his famed Delta Lines O scale layout, **7-23**. Featured in an article that appeared in the August 1952 issue of *Toy Trains* magazine, the building was built out of illustration board.

7-23

Pioneer model railroader Frank Ellison would be proud of this present-day resin re-creation of his original cardstock model.

7-24

You'll often find flash along edges and in open areas of a resin casting. Always use a sharp blade in your hobby knife to remove flash.

7-25

It's important to keep the wall perpendicular to the sandpaper when truing up an edge. Work slowly—a little sanding goes a long way.

7-26

I carried the cornice across the back wall, so I didn't have to cut into the roof line. The mismatched alignment isn't noticeable in the finished model.

7-27

The wall is masked in preparation for spraying the windows and doors. Blue painter's tape facilitates the masking process.

Resin kits are really no more difficult to put together than a plastic-injection molded kit. In fact, this particular kit is on par with an Ameri-Towne or Korber kit in terms of assembly. However, after reading the instructions and looking over the parts, I decided to alter the kit, which is no big surprise since I can't ever leave anything alone. What bothered me about the kit was the lack of space above the windows on the side walls, which I'll get back to in a bit.

On resin castings, you may find flash along the edges, especially in the window openings, and, in this particular kit, on the loading dock support, **7-24**. I removed the flash with a sharp knife blade, following up with a small file and sandpaper.

Next, I test-fit the walls. The corners should mate without any apparent seam. Both mating surfaces as well as the wall bottoms should be flat and straight. When truing up an edge, I always work slowly and frequently check the fit—a little sanding goes a long way, **7-25**. You may also need to sand the backs of the front and rear walls. Holding them against a metal straightedge will tell you if they need some work.

With the basics out of the way, I tackled the side-wall modification. I decided to add a ¼"-wide cornice to each side wall. So the roof lines would match, the back wall also needed to be raised. To do so, I followed an architectural convention by simply carrying the cornice across the back wall. That entailed cutting the wall apart and inserting the cornice between the two pieces, **7-26**. I stacked two pieces of strip styrene (.030" x .250" and .125" x .250") to make the cornice. This allowed the cornice to be flush with the cast-in trim pieces.

The wall was separated along the board line immediately above the window. I carefully scored a groove along that line, using the back of my hobby knife blade, which took several passes. Then, I carried the line onto the raised trim on each side as a guide for the finishing saw cut, which I did with a fine-tooth blade. After cleaning up the cuts, I laid the pieces facedown on a glass cutting board and carefully lined everything up. I then used CA to bond the styrene to the resin walls.

As mentioned previously, I find it much easier to paint walls having cast-in details before final assembly. For me, the ease of manipulating a single wall piece while spray painting far outweighs having to scrape paint from a mating surface before gluing. Even if you have to touch up a painted surface afterward, it's no big deal. But more importantly, the first step in obtaining a great paint job on both plastic and resin is cleaning off the mold-release compound and any oils from handling. I can't stress this enough.

With the prep work done, I sprayed the walls with several light coats of white primer. I let that dry for the minimum recommended time before painting the trim with Krylon Khaki Camouflage. With as many windows as there are in these walls, brush-painting would be tedious at best, so I opted to mask the wall, **7-27**.

This is not as time-consuming as you might think. I use blue painter's tape because its low adhesion makes it ideal for this purpose, and it will not take off paint as regular masking tape can do. The blue painter's tape is also very thin, which makes it easy to press on for a tight fit. I first applied horizontal strips of tape across the wall, adjacent to the window and door tops and bottoms. I then ran the 1"-wide tape vertically, tearing it lengthwise to fit the spaces. Finally, I filled in any uncovered spots. The process took about five minutes per wall and greatly simplified painting the windows and trim. To spray each side, I simply rotated the wall, and it was done.

Assembly is straightforward. On kits like this, I like to use bar clamps and a corner clamp to keep the walls in perfect alignment, **7-28**. I applied a drop of CA at the top of the inside corner and let it run down, so it would wick into the seam via capillary action. I'll often use a toothpick to move it along, and if necessary, I'll add another drop where the first one stops. I repeated the process on the remaining two walls and then joined the two halves together, placing them on a glass cutting board, **7-29**. Because the glass is perfectly flat, the cutting board assures an even base.

As the final step, I added the roof sections but not before coloring them, **7-30**. I sprayed them with flat white primer and then gave them successive washes with my India ink and alcohol weathering solution. This takes some time since you have to let it dry between washes, but it's time well spent since the end result is so realistic.

White Tower restaurant craftsman kit

This is a neat, little O scale plastic craftsman kit by Twin Whistle Sign & Kit Company (www.twinwhistle.com), **7-31**. Yet, upon opening this kit box, you're likely to hear yourself utter

7-28

A corner clamp on the bottom and a bar clamp on the top assure a perfect alignment prior to gluing. The strip of plastic between the sidewall and the corner clamp, which matches the thickness of the window trim, keeps the wall perpendicular. This process is repeated on the other two walls.

7-29

Bar clamps, a carpenter's square, and a glass cutting board keep the structure's walls straight and true.

7-30

Roof weathering doesn't get any better than this, and it couldn't be easier. The white-primed roof was repeatedly washed with an India ink and alcohol weathering solution.

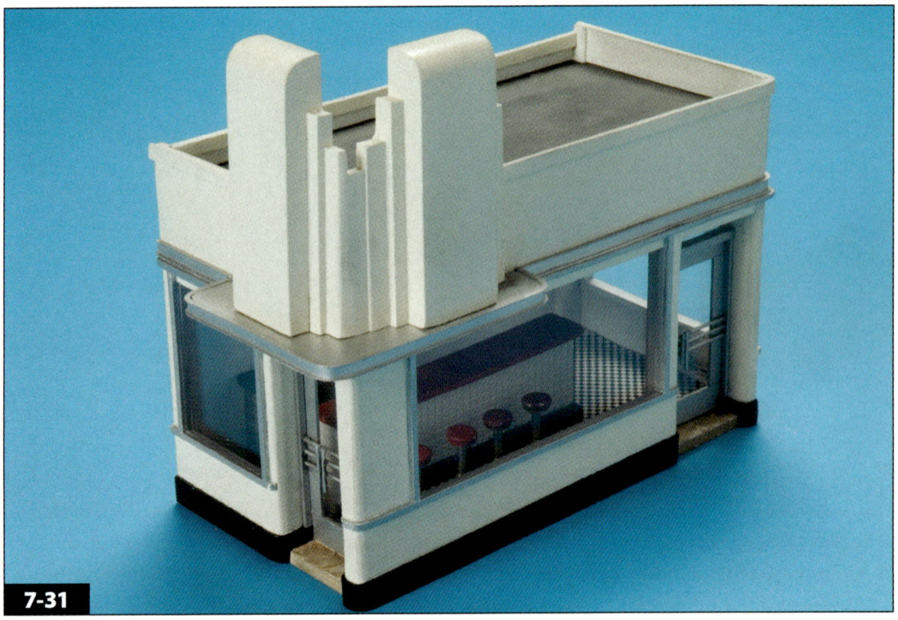

7-31

This White Tower restaurant, a plastic craftsman kit by Twin Whistle Sign & Kit Company, was improved by adding several details.

7-32

Identifying and laying out the parts helps you understand where the pieces go and how they fit together.

7-33

I made a custom decorative edge piece that joined the upper and lower sections. This was an improvement over the original kit design.

"yikes!" That's because you're faced with an assortment of flat plastic pieces, a few resin castings, and some miscellaneous detail parts. But don't let that scare you—once you get into it, it's really not all that difficult.

After identifying and laying out the precut parts, **7-32**, I decided to make a custom T-shaped piece to fit between the upper and lower sections of the front and side walls. The instructions called for butting the pieces together and then adding a strip edgewise to cover the seam and create a small decorative ledge. While this would work, it doesn't add much to the building's structural integrity. My simple modification keeps the overhang and disguises the seam at the same time. It also provides a straight edge and a solid backing for joining the separate pieces, **7-33**. Before adding the insert piece, I bonded the bottom pieces with their uprights, using a carpenter's square for alignment.

Once the front and the side walls were completed, I assembled the basic structure as I normally do, first joining two sides together and then the two halves. If the corners are square, the building will be square, **7-34**.

After the four walls were joined, I rounded the exterior corners with a large, flexible nail file. I also added a few decorative pieces not included in the original kit, **7-35**. These simple little details enhanced an otherwise plain facade. My inspiration came from several

White Tower restaurant details

Evergreen Scale Models strip styrene

No.	Size	Detail
136	.030" x .125"	Interior window frame for depth
138	.030" x .188"	Door top and sides
139	.030" x .250"	Door bottom and black wall trim
143	.040" x .060"	Door and window trim
146	.040" x .125"	Top wall trim
154	.060" x .080"	Top door trim
189	.125" x .250"	Concrete steps and interior bracing
264	⅛" x .125"	Decorative silver molding above insert piece
295	5/32" x .156"	Custom angled insert piece

places, including a model by Mike Tylick in a 1997 Walthers Big Trains catalog. I also did an Internet search for White Tower photos and found what appeared to be the sources for both the kit and Mike's model.

Placing the glossy, black tile strip along the bottom was a bit tricky where it makes a 180-degree bend on left side of each doorway. The trick here is to use a full-length strip allowing it to overhang at each end. Once glued, I trimmed it to fit. Before making the bend, I held the strip flat against the inside of the doorway, applied liquid plastic cement, and let it dry. I then applied more cement as I slowly bent it around the curve and worked my way to the other door. The glue softens the plastic, allowing you to make the bend. If you go too fast, it will snap. When that happened to me, I simply butted it up, applied more glue, and continued. Similarly, I added a decorative trim piece along the top of the front and side walls.

After applying the window trim, I added interior bracing along the bottom of the walls, **7-36**. This also provides a firm frame under the floor and allowed me to add a concrete step in each doorway.

I then sprayed the building, inside and out, with white primer. After that dried, I masked the back of openings and applied an off-white satin paint. This imparted a faded appearance to the exterior while leaving the inside bright white. The black strip was painted after masking the rest of the building.

To give the canopy a more substantial look, I added the ⅛" channel to its outside perimeter and then trimmed it to fit. I sprayed the canopy silver before attaching it to the building with CA. Instant-setting glue is a good choice here for bonding painted plastic. Now, with the canopy in place, I continued the prepainted channel across the front and side walls.

I substituted .060" clear acrylic sheet for the plastic glazing included with the kit. Besides reinforcing the model, it allowed me to build the doors in place.

Once you have the basics down for building different types of kits, you can try your hand at kitbashing, which I'll describe in the book's final chapter.

7-34

A machinist's square and a carpenter's square keep the sides straight while you apply the glue.

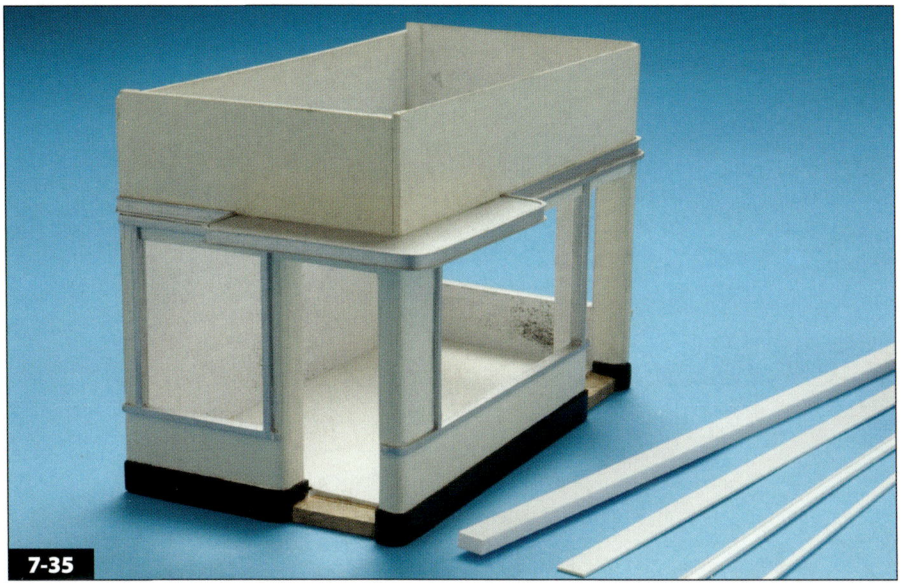

7-35

Rounding the corners and adding a few trim pieces add extra dimension and enhance the kit's plain exterior.

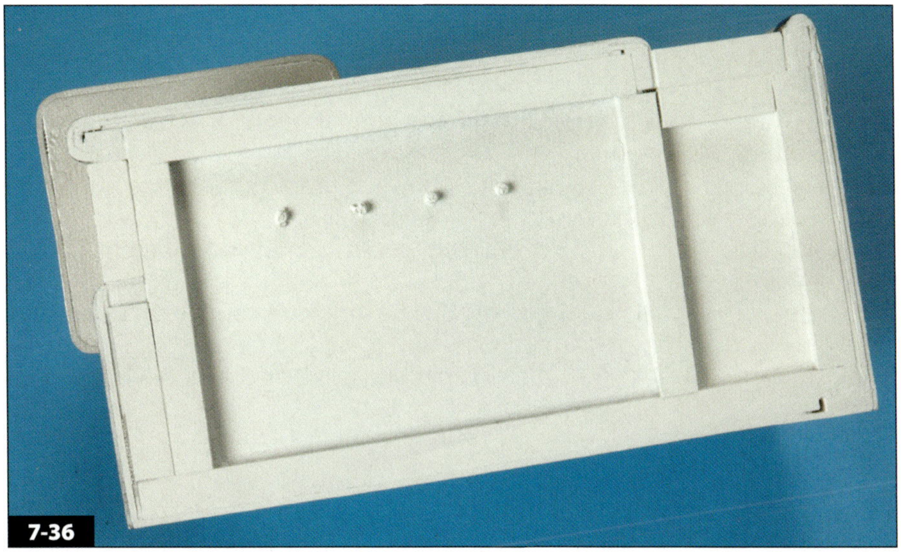

7-36

To make the thin plastic walls and floor more rigid, you can add interior bracing at the bottom of the building.

8-1

Kitbashing 101

The sounds reverberate through the industrial canyon as the little steamer rumbles through on well-pounded rails past a variety of kitbashed buildings.

Kitbashing is often thought of as using two or more of the same kits to enlarge a building. But kitbashed projects can range from modifying the parts of just a single kit to combining pieces from several different kits to make an entirely unique structure. Kitbashing can be simple or complex, it's up to you. And it doesn't only apply to buildings. Almost anything can be kitbashed—bridges, railroad cars, engines, and accessories.

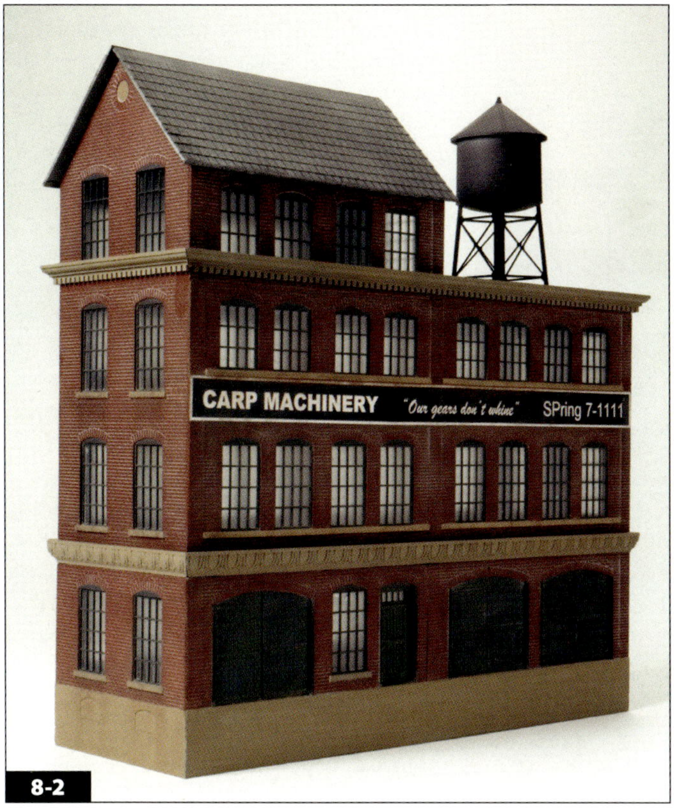

8-2

It took four kits to make Carp Machinery. Paying attention to detail and following standard architectural conventions produced a realistic early 20th century factory.

8-3

Many old industrial buildings exhibit the decorative architectural flourishes common in the early 1900s. Note the three windows between the pillars on the upper floors.

About 80 percent of the buildings on the Sandy Harbor have been altered in some way, **8-1**, but most viewers would never know it. And that's the way it should be. A successful kitbash shouldn't give itself away. There is a definite art to it, but once you know the basics, you'll be well on your way to kitbashing success. Here are four important fundamentals:

- Pick the right kit for the job. Some kits work better for expanding a building's footprint rather than being stacked to gain height.
- Look for kits with repeating patterns. These are well suited for making larger structures, whether stacked or expanding a footprint.
- Use a scanner or a copier to make paper printouts of walls and other components. Cut and paste these pieces together in order to figure out various possibilities. You can then use them as templates.
- Make your cuts where they will be the least noticeable. Remember, this is plastic surgery. You may not be able to eliminate the scars, but you can minimize them by concealing them in a natural joint such as a corner.

8-4

Decorative molding sets off the first floor of this building from the other stories. If applied judiciously, signs and graffiti are interesting details to add to a model.

I wrestled with how to present this chapter on kitbashing. I could've given you detailed step-by-step instructions for constructing numerous buildings. But a big problem with that approach is that some kits are no longer in production. So where would you go from there? Instead, I'll present detailed descriptions of how I kitbashed Carp Machinery and the freight house, which employ several basic techniques that you should know. Then, I'll give broader examples of various other kitbashing techniques. These builds will explain the kitbashing process and provide a blueprint for guiding you through your own creative discoveries.

8-5

I used Lionel municipal building and electrical substation kits in the kitbash of Carp Machinery. Although they're no longer in production, you can find the kits online or at swap meets.

8-6

Building a mockup is a great way to work out the design of a complex kitbash. I used this basic design but later changed the loading dock door configuration.

8-7

These are two of the four kit wall configurations that make up Carp Machinery's long walls. Notice the short windows on the second stories.

8-8

Of the kit side walls, the red brick wall proved to be most useful because of the extra rows of bricks below the roof line.

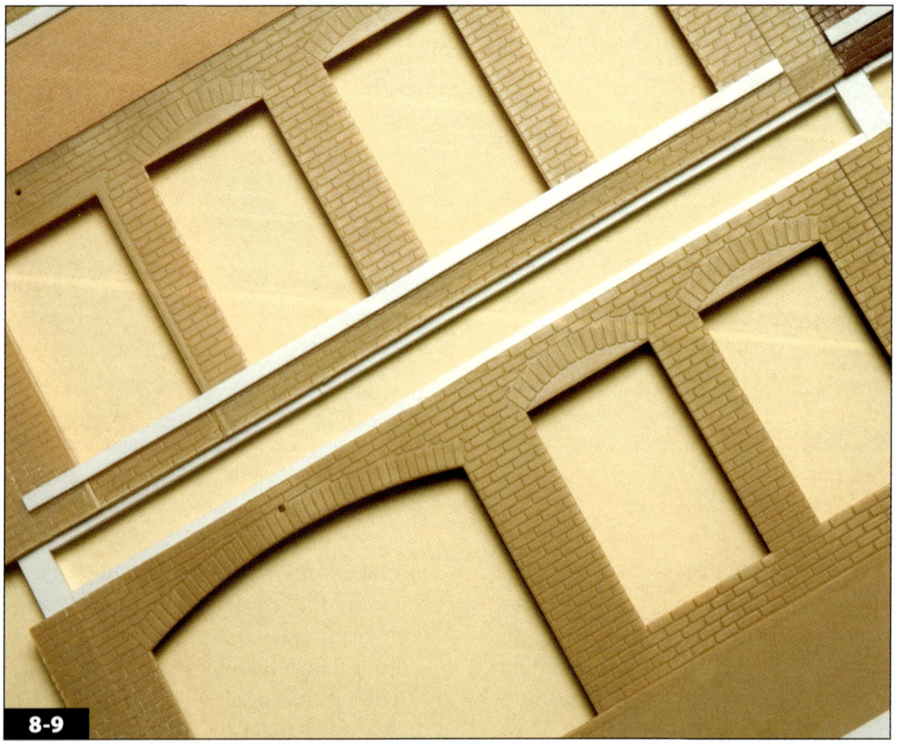

8-9

I used styrene strips as a backing for the decorative molding and also for the windowsills. Inserting a brick piece under the far-left opening helps turn a door into a window.

Remember, the most important tool in your toolbox is not one that you can buy in a store, it's your imagination. As you look at kits, think outside their boxes and experiment with all the possibilities.

Carp Machinery

Carp Machinery is a perfect example of how to kitbash a building with a repeating pattern. It also represents an architectural style common to commercial structures at the beginning of the 20th century, **8-2**. These buildings sport brick pillars across their facade and have one or more windows between the pillars, **8-3**. Often, they have decorative molding between the first and second stories, **8-4**.

To make this building, I used two each of Lionel's electric substation (6-12931) and municipal building (6-22915) kits, **8-5**. Their wall sections are interchangeable, and although modified, they appear to come from the same molds. Oftentimes, successive kits will use the same castings, possibly with some alterations, from previous releases. That's something to look for when buying kits from the same manufacturer. For a kitbasher, this provides additional building options.

Creating a mockup is a crucial step in a complex kitbash, **8-6**. When producing printouts of parts, make several copies of each piece, so you can try various configurations. Be sure to label the printouts, so you know which kit components they match.

The two Lionel kits use the same front and back walls although they have different door and window placements, **8-7**. The side walls differ as one has a squared-off roof line with a truncated peak, **8-8**. While these castings are nice, there is a problem—the floors are too close together. There's no room for floor joists between stories. Even though the joists are not visible, you have to allow for them or the structure looks odd. It was precisely that anomaly that led to Carp Machinery's distinctive look.

To solve that problem, I cut the walls horizontally in line with the bottom edge of the small windows. This allowed me to add a realistic space between the floors to compensate for the shortcoming in the castings—hence, the decorative molding above the first floor, **8-9**. To keep the spacing uniform between the next two floors, I added a

8-10

I cut the stock walls apart horizontally in order to place the short windows on the third and fourth floors. The short windows have been cut along the bottom of their openings, leaving a strip of bricks above the windows on the second story. Wooden, dentil crown dollhouse molding, 1"-wide stripwood, and shelf molding fill the spaces.

8-11

Signs between floors are common on commercial structures. The building looks different above the fourth floor, so it's possible that the top three floors were added later.

8-12

The windows in the top two floors of this seed wholesaler are smaller than the rest. There is only one window between the pillars. Note the corrugated metal roof above the concrete loading dock.

8-13

Looking at the structural skeleton, it's quite obvious where the horizontal seams are located. The vertical pieces of styrene add support and help join the pieces.

1"-wide basswood strip mounted flush with the bricks. This strip also served as backing for the company sign, **8-10**. These signs often appeared between floors on commercial buildings, **8-11**.

Finally, a strip of wooden dentil crown molding capped the third-story roof and provided separation for the fourth floor. I also altered the window configuration by placing the smaller windows on the upper two floors. This, too, is prototypical, **8-12**.

Expanding the building's footprint was a simple matter of removing the column from each adjoining wall section, thereby maintaining the column width between sets of windows. This also neatly disguised the seams by placing them at natural joints in the brickwork.

I carefully assembled the walls using a straightedge since keeping everything plumb is especially important in this type of project. I used .125" x .250" Evergreen strip styrene as a backing for the molding and to hold everything together, **8-13**.

A door does not always have to be a door—it can be a window and vice versa. Unless I wanted to buy another kit, I had to use a section with a door and three windows on one of the upper stories. What do you do with the door? This is not an uncommon problem in a kitbash. Typically, I will block in the space with concrete-painted plastic and then add a vent of some sort. This is also very common, especially in old brick buildings. It's far easier to exhaust a piece of machinery through a blocked-up window opening than by punching a hole through four or more layers of brick.

In this case, however, the width of the door opening matched that of the window, so I simply put a window in its place, **8-14**. Of course, then I had to add a strip of brick underneath the window. The brick strip came from a window that I turned into a door, **8-15**.

Carp Machinery shows how you can take a problem and turn it into an opportunity to create a unique structure. It was a challenge, but for me, that's part of the fun.

The freight house

This model was inspired by photos of the New York Central freight house on Manhattan's west side (see photo **6-2**

8-14 It's evident in this closeup that the left window treatment is different from its neighbor, but no one ever notices. That's because I didn't do anything to draw attention to it. Even on prototypes, you'll find variations that go unnoticed by the casual observer, so this is not without precedence.

8-15 Turning a window into a door is as simple as cutting out the bricks below the window. I also added plastic angle pieces on each side of the door to represent metal corner guards. The window glass is frosted on the inside with Krylon clear matte spray.

Freight house materials list

Kits

5 Plasticville Airport Hanger kits (6-45986)

(one kit for the front wall, one for the back, and three for the third story walls)

Wall and corner seams

Plastruct AFS-8 ¼" styrene angle

Plastruct CFS-8 ¼" styrene channel

Side roof support

Evergreen .060" x .125" strip styrene

Evergreen .040" x .125" strip styrene

Interior seams

Evergreen .080" x .250" strip styrene

Evergreen 3/16" square tube strip styrene)

Roof covering

Black construction paper

Corrugated side walls

20" x 30" sheet of 3/16" black foam board

Corrugated scrapbooking material (groove spacing 1/8" center to center)

or 5 Evergreen 6" x 12" .125" corrugated siding sheets

Window glazing

Translucent, flexible plastic cutting board

Miscellaneous

Plastruct ABS HR-8 handrail (O scale)

Plastruct KL-8 ladder (O scale)

8-16 The dockworker is dwarfed by the freight house and surrounding buildings in a scene that could be taken right out of *On the Waterfront*.

on page 57). I say inspired because it's not a scale reproduction by any means. Yet, it is remarkably evocative of the warehouses found on the piers along the Hudson River, **8-16**. That's the beauty of using modeler's license—a successful model only needs to capture the essence or flavor of the original.

Even when told this is a bashed model, hardly anyone recognizes that the windowed walls came from Plasticville airplane hanger kits, **8-17**, or that the fluted sides started out as corrugated cardboard. This building is what I call a *scratchbash*—part scratchbuilt, part kitbash. I used five kits to make this building. The airplane hanger kits came to mind because of the windows. I had previously purchased them at a train show, thinking they would be good fodder for bashing. When the need for a freight house cropped up, I knew that I had the right ingredients. I used two hanger back walls (top) and 10 side walls in the construction of the freight house.

The most critical part of the freight house's construction was determining the width of the rail car opening. Because

8-17

The smooth, shiny Plasticville Airplane Hanger is a neat toy train accessory but hardly ever considered as an ingredient for a kitbash.

8-18

The end walls are assembled and primed. Capping the ends with L channel makes the walls appear thicker. The U channel effectively covers the seams.

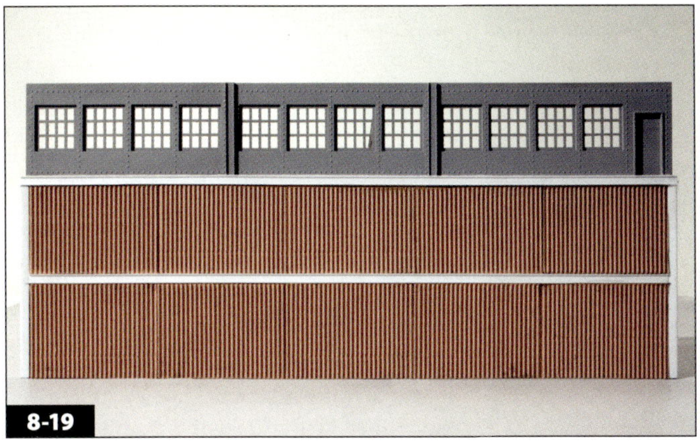

8-19

Three side walls make up the clerestory's rear side wall. One wall is intact while the other two have lost their doors. Seams are hidden by styrene channel pieces.

8-20

Since I may detail the interior in the future, I used the original interlocking corner tabs to hold the rear side wall in position.

it had to fit behind the gantry crane and straddle a siding, it was going to be a tight fit. So the first order of business was putting the end walls together, **8-18**. First, I eliminated the doors from the stock walls by cutting alongside the door frame. The key here is to maintain the symmetry of the windows with respect to the left and right ends of the wall. This is especially important when assembling the clerestory (the upper area with windows on the long side wall above the roof).

The top row of front windows is slightly offset from the windows below it. If I had more space, I would have been able to keep the two outside top windows in line with the bottom inside windows. If it was a larger structure, you could easily add a wing on the other side and then center the roof.

I then assembled the rear side wall, **8-19**. Again, the wall's length was determined by what would fit in the available space. I ended up using one stock wall having a door and two walls without doors. I didn't give the door on this wall any special treatment. Since it's not easily viewable, I just let it be, and who knows why it's there? The corrugated part of the wall was backed with black foam board, which is a bit denser than regular white foam core. To simulate the metal siding, I used a package of corrugated cardboard pieces that I picked up in the scrapbook aisle of a craft store. You could easily substitute Evergreen corrugated siding sheets. The seams are hidden beneath a Plastruct ¼" styrene channel. This design element is found on the prototype and ties in very nicely with the riveted, metal-clad kit walls. You'll notice that I used this artifice throughout.

I bonded the corrugated cardboard to its foam-board backing with 3M Super 77 spray adhesive and used cyanoacrylate adhesive (CA) to attach the styrene channel to the foam. On the dock-side corrugated wall, I cut out two large entryways.

Before assembling the four walls, I placed styrene strips on the interior as a backing for the joints and to add structural integrity, **8-20**.

After painting the walls, I fashioned Evergreen styrene strips into roof supports. Besides adding rigidity, the supports tied the clerestory and the wall together, **8-21**.

The access door to the roof creates a little visual relief in the front, **8-22**. Having a door on the clerestory level suggests a catwalk inside, which is typical of a freight house like this.

Adding the roof capped off this project. To get the correct size, I used a full hanger roof at each end and cut a third to fit between them, **8-23**. I glued white styrene strips to the edge of the two outside roof sections, **8-24**. This provided

8-21

This closeup shows how the support structure ties the wall to the clerestory. Since I already painted the walls, I used cyanoacrylate adhesive to attach these pieces.

8-22

A neat little detail like this doorway offers more than what you see, suggesting that something lies behind it. Surely, there must be a catwalk and a ladder leading up to it inside.

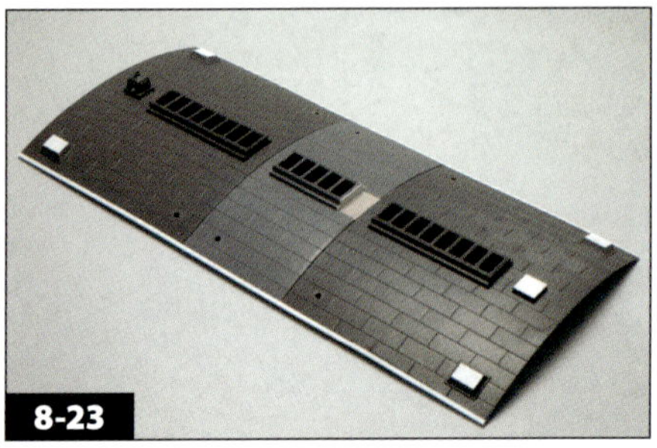

8-23

This shows how the middle roof section was cut to fit. I made a new end for the shortened skylight and plugged the remaining hole with a piece of styrene.

8-24

The styrene strips are first attached to the inside ends of the full roof sections. These lips will support the cut-down middle section.

8-25

The roofing sheets have started to come up and will have to be reattached with spray glue.

support and a lip for attaching the center section to the others.

To simulate rolled roofing, I applied strips of black construction paper using rubber cement as the adhesive. This turned out to not be a good idea. The roofing is starting to come loose, **8-25**, so I will have to reattach it with spray glue. Weathering the roof was easy. Once it was attached, I rubbed gray chalk across its surface.

The freight house was a much simpler build than Carp Machinery but no less satisfying. Could more details have been added? Certainly, and I'll most probably add things like lights, downspouts, and perhaps a vent or two. But even without those refinements, the building is a fine representation. If you start with broad strokes, the fine details can be filled in later.

Kitbashing techniques

Carp Machinery is an excellent example of making a building with a repeating pattern, and the freight house uses a similar construction technique. But not all kits lend themselves to that approach. Recognizing a kit for its potential is something that comes with experience and a bit of luck. I've broken some common kitbashing methods into general categories, but the truth is that there's a lot of crossover. The examples on the following pages give an overview of these kitbashing techniques and provide a look at a variety of possibilities.

Adding on

Another way to alter a kit is to attach an obvious addition, which gives a sense of expansion over time Although no less creative, this is probably the easiest type of kitbash. Regardless of the original building's style, the add-on can be constructed from any material. Nothing has to match and that's the beauty of it. The real skill is in making the addition seem plausible.

Ranberg Foundry
The old MTH granary building begged for an addition or two, and I was only too happy to oblige. The story goes that the original owner went out of business and sold the building. The new company needed a large boiler and built the cinder-block annex to house it.

The cinder-block boiler house walls came from the lower half of a Lionel coaling station kit (6-12904). The roof is a piece of Evergreen corrugated siding. I cut the foundation from an HO concrete retaining wall and scratchbuilt the porch from styrene. I made the chimney from a length of ½" plastic water pipe and scored the joints with a pipe cutter. The flange at the base is the center of an old radio knob. Guy wires made of black thread are attached to eye pins.

I imagine the loading dock was partially enclosed at some point to provide a place to store outgoing shipments and keep them out of the weather. The dock supports, the board-and-batten enclosure, and the roof came from an old Lionel freight platform kit (6-12773). I used scale lumber for the deck.

Alcoa
Sometimes a facility acquires such a hodgepodge of additions that the original structure gets lost in the maze. The Alcoa complex fits into this category. I rearranged the walls of two different Walthers kits to make this conglomeration. The wedged-shaped structure and the building on the riser come from the American Hardware Supply kit (933-3097), and the other buildings are made from a George Roberts Printing Company kit (933-3046).

Expanding the footprint

Instead of going up, you can also go out by expanding a building's footprint. This is usually somewhat easier than stacking. A vertical seam can be hidden in a corner or simply covered with a downspout or vent pipe. As you'll see, I like the corner approach.

Adam Metal Supply
Walthers Red Wing Milling Co. (933-3026) is another good candidate for expansion. I used a full side wall on the right and took the cut section from the back corner. This pattern can be reversed, and the main viewing angle will determine which way to orient the jog. I didn't paint the foam core wall since it can't be seen.

Rumie Roller Bearing Co.
I reversed the pattern on Walthers Northern Light & Power powerhouse (933-3021) because the main viewing angle comes from the opposite direction. Notice that the windows are centered within the strip.

National Cold Storage
Walthers Champion packing plant (933-3048) is a great example of a kit that is best suited for expanding a footprint. The zigzag pattern is one that I frequently use when combining a front and back wall side by side. It adds relief to the facade and hides the seam with minimal surgery. This is a great technique for making background flats. To do this, I cut off a narrow strip from one of the building's side walls and used it to make a jog in the footprint. As you can see, I cut the strip from the left back corner. This little trick provides a perfectly matched outside corner joint and places the cut edge on the inside corner where it's less obvious.

Stacking for height

Stacking kits for height should be as easy as it sounds—stacking building sections on top of each other. Ah, but there's the rub—disguising horizontal seams and maintaining consistent floor spacing may sometimes require a bit of ingenuity as you've seen with Carp Machinery.

Dorable Doll Corp.
Even plaster kits can be kitbashed. The Dorable Doll Corp. is made from stacked window sections salvaged from two 3-story building fronts. These sections are chipped, broken, or otherwise imperfect castings left over from a Universal Supply kit, and they're fine for background buildings. I used white glue to bond them to a solid foam core backing. The window inserts are thin, brown cardboard. For the building next door, I used a side wall from the kit as its back wall with the kit's back wall becoming the building's side wall. The window inserts are corrugated cardboard. A foam core wall separates the buildings.

Allied Paper
Believe it or not, this is a kitbash of four Plasticville apartment buildings (no. 45980) on top of a foam core loading dock. As you can see in the rear view, there was quite a bit of surgery done to this one. I cut the double-windowed side walls in half, which left me with extra windows that I used in the indented center section. The original kit has the same shape, but the center section contained a door and a window. I cut the entire center section out and replaced it with two separate side-wall window sections. I covered the horizontal seams with styrene strips and added a downspout from a Walthers HO refinery piping kit. The loading dock is painted foam core, and its door is a Grandt Line product.

N. B. Sougloff Corp.
This building breaks away from my practice of keeping consistent spacing between floors. I simply stacked one wall on top of another without any modification. This left a double-wide concrete beam running horizontally across the building. I did this, so I could make the sign larger. The sign looks perfectly natural and keeps you from noticing what I did. It is kitbashed from Walthers George Roberts Printing (933-3046) and Variety Printing (933-3252) kits.

TSB Industries
Nothing fancy here. I stacked the front and side walls of Wathers Front Street warehouse (933-3069) to make this six-story building. The only modification I did was to remove the foundation from the upper walls. I made one side wall out of foam core because it is mostly hidden from view. It can only be seen from a distance at the far end of the layout, and from that vantage point, its mottled color looks like brick.

Andrew Roger Manufacturing
The front, back, and side walls were stacked to make this five-story structure from a Walthers REA transfer building (933-3095). It also has a foam core wall painted to suggest brick when viewed from a distance. This background building sits on a riser behind other buildings, so it looks even taller.

Shape to fit

Commercial property in industrial areas comes at a premium, so no space gets wasted. Often, you may end up with an odd-shaped space, so you have to build to fit it.

Eastern Tool
Such is the case with this little triangular gem in the midst of the harbor district. It was created from the leftover pieces of an O scale Walthers Brook Hill Farm Dairy (933-3305) employed in a previous kitbash. I used Evergreen sheet styrene to build the curved concrete loading dock and made the roof from Evergreen corrugated styrene. The board-and-batten addition came from a Lionel freight station kit (6-12773).

Repeating patterns

Here are several more examples of creating buildings that have a repeating pattern.

Gateway Chemical
Located in the background, the Gateway Chemical Company started out as a single-story Lionel factory building. Kits like this can easily be expanded to fill any size footprint without any modification. The building is made up of overlapping brick sections, and adding height is a simple matter of cutting off the base and stacking the walls. Just because background buildings are not as prominent, they don't have to be flat. The four-story tower, second-story roof, stairwell entry, ladder, and vent provide lots of detail without being overdone.

Unlimited Plastics
Lionel offered this as a single-stall engine house. It, too, consists of overlapping sections, only they were two panels wide. Nevertheless, I cut them apart to change their configuration. Like the factory kit, each section has a raised brick pattern surrounding the windows. I turned it into a concrete beam and brick building by covering the raised bricks with drywall joint compound.

Westside Apartments
Here is a repeating pattern of a different sort. I combined seven HO City Classics commercial building kits. Although the kits in this series had different fronts, I only used the backs and the sides. This was a very easy build. I put together four 3-sided buildings and inserted a back wall between each one. Older buildings often have staggered walls to allow additional daylight to enter through the side windows.

About the author

In putting this book together, Dennis Brennan has combined several of his interests. An avid model railroader for more than 30 years, he especially enjoys making scenery and kitbashing structures. Dennis is also a commercial photographer, and his photos have appeared in *Classic Toy Trains*, *Model Railroader*, and *O Gauge Railroading*. He has contributed numerous articles to CTT, and his four-part series on the Sandy Harbor Terminal Ry. appeared in the December 2007 to March 2008 issues.

In his spare time, Dennis is a professional scenery builder and modeler. He also runs Brennan's Model Railroading Products. In another life, Dennis directed TV commercials, industrial films, television shows, and music videos. He graduated from Rutgers University.

Dennis lives in Independence, Mo., with his wife Sandy and Madigan, their wire-haired dachshund mix. Dennis and Sandy have three children: Tyler, Dorian, and Leah.

Dedication

This book is dedicated to my wife, Sandy, whose loving support and encouragement, and the fact that she has a real job, made all of this possible.

Acknowledgements

Many people helped me, directly and indirectly, with the Sandy Harbor Terminal Ry. including Rick Banta, Richard Farmer, Eric Green, Pat Hennebery, Dave Jacobs, Frank Knautz, Curt Kneisley, Lloyd Turpin, Al Zamorski as well as my friends at Atlas O and those at Kalmbach Publishing.

And a special thanks to my dear friend and fellow artist, Roberta Moog, who taught me "If you can envision it, you can do it."